FISHERS
OF
TROUT
AND
MEN:

Protectors Of The Realm

Richard C. Raugust

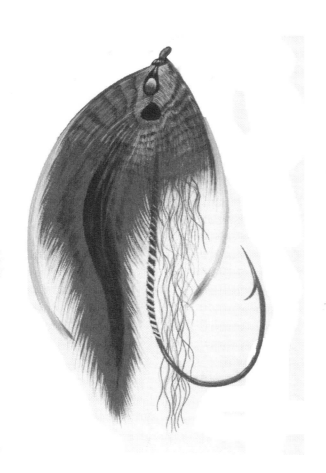

DEDICATION

This national treasure is dedicated to my grandfather, Craig W. Reese, infantry soldier with the WWII 104th. Inf. Division, a.k.a., "Timberwolves," trout fishing instructor extraordinaire, and to (all) soldiers who have answered the country's call in every MOS, as well as to (all) lovers of the intangible who lead by example, past, present, and future—whenever they can and wherever they happen to roam.

May these stories entertain, enlighten, and console the entire human race, encouraging us all to do more than our part while upholding realms unknown.

AUSPICIOUS SIGNS
R.C.R. 11B
Fisher Of Trout And Men

SPECIAL THANKS

I would like to especially thank Marci Jones and Mary Webster for their years of support, without which this collection might not have been possible.

Also, these friends deserve a Huge round of applause, as they believed in my position and donned their capes to solve my caper: Brenden McQuillan; Jessie McQuillan; Spencer Veysey; Toby Cook; Sarah Ferguson; Jeff Patterson, creator of *From Herd 2 Human* and owner of Willowbend Farm; the Montana Innocence Project; as well as these attorneys from the Missoula Law Firm of Tipp & Buley: Bryan Tipp, Brett Schandelson & Sarah Lockwood, who spent many hundreds of hours researching, investigating, and presenting the evidence in a manner that led to my release. The legal team that came together to shed the light of day on this tragedy are some of the finest people on the planet and would stand with the best in any courtroom!

A special thought I send out to Maria Raugust, my dream, my gift, my wife. Just when I thought finding The One was a futile endeavor, my gift wrapped in a blessing magically appeared. Thanks for everything, Baby!

I would also like to mention the love and warmth shared with me by my daughter Audrey and son Kevi, who allow this poet to love them unconditionally and bless my life every day I am in their presence.

Let me not forget Mr. Dan Weinberg, the dreamer, creator and founder of the Montana Innocence Project. Without his brilliant oversight and vision, I would still be existing in a living hell.

And to everyone else who helped support my voracious appetite for books, and little things that made life bearable... we know who you are!

bravo

AUTHOR'S NOTE

Welcome!

You are about to enter into a realm of unimaginable delights, a small gift meant to enlighten your mind and lighten your load.

The tales told in these pages are a direct, real, and contemplative experience of the author who has spent countless hours in the wild chasing elusive rainbows and many months at the fort where hundreds of thousands of men and women have trained to answer the call of duty. Harmony Church is where I got my dirty boots.

It is the intention of this collection that, as lovers of adventure and the great outdoors, we will use our predisposition to action for the greater good.

As you will read, there is a slightly heavy mystical-otherworldly tone to many of these pieces, a result of cosmic battles hard to fathom. My tour at the fort sure served me well! Whatever path you have chosen makes not a lot of difference, as long as you aim for peace and compassion as the ultimate goal. If you have worn a uniform in one of the armed services from around the globe, you are uniquely qualified and highly sought after by invisible forces spoken about or alluded to in this thin book.

We are all on this blue planet travelling through eternity together and the sooner we realize that there is much more to life and the fabric of reality we all experience on a daily basis, the sooner we will wake up and unite as brothers and sisters in a very concerted effort to save this magical gift.

Get ready to enjoy the ride you are about to depart upon, and when you have returned from this little journey, please try and live up to your potential while making a **&%$##@!! difference before it's too late!

Till The Reels Fall Off,
R.C.R. —2016

charlie

FISHERS OF TROUT AND MEN:
Protectors Of The Realm

Table of Delights

1	FISHERS OF TROUT AND MEN
2	Heaven's Reward / Blow Your Mind / Friendly Thud
3	Salt & Pepper / Wherever It's Found / Hide And Seek
4	Plenty Left / In Public / Things Behind
5	NEVER SEEN
6	Ancient Sage / Presentation / Ten Thousand Doors
7	Big Bows / Polishing My Mirror / Some Good
8	The Undercut / Drop The Fly / Trout Lies
9	WHAT CAN YOU DO?
10	Prime Run / Glassy Water / Inner Life
11	Blue Planet / Proud To Be / Something To Grasp
12	Constant Change / Favorite Stream / About To Begin
13	AS IT STANDS NOW
14	Daily Rounds / Troubled Minds / Nothing To Compare
15	Returning Home / In Remembrance / Try To Make Sense
16	Your Life / Take Your Seats / Little Castle
17	MAKE THE RIGHT DECISION
18	Feed Lane / Deception And Guile / Reely Scream
19	Another Tour / Inner Eye / River Calls
20	Yellow Moon / The Puzzle / Realms Unknown
21	FORT BENNING
22	Luckiest Soul / Forgiven / Be Who You Are
23	Little Book / Sport And Adventure / Next Formation
24	Patience And Wisdom / Graphite Whip / The Way
25	SECRET HOLE
26	Fisher Of Men / Another Shot / Vigor And Life
27	Things To Come / Seek And Roam / Eye To Eye

28   My Dreams / Perfect Show / To Be Desired

29   IT COULD BE HAD

30   Now Gone / Tame And Conquer / Warmed Up

31   Had To Be Done / Heaven's Door / Ride The Currents

32   While I Dance / Stir The Fire / Mission's Done

33   COSMIC EMBRACE

34   Long White Robes / With Nary A Care / Nothing But

35   Ain't Easy / White Crane / Making Noise

36   From The Capitol / Straight And Narrow / Dope I Prefer

37   STEWARDS OF THE PLANET

38   Never Saying No / Check The Fridge / My Buddies

39   Splitting Jokes / Where I Go / No Claim

40   Ancient Domain / Clinging / Start Again

41   SAME OLD STORY

42   Pay Us Back / Soon Enough / Little Finger

43   Memories / I'm Lucky / Tested And True

44   S.A.W. / Dimple Her Water / Fat Lips

45   GO TO THE WATER

46   Duet / Next Move / More Often

47   Long Throw / Slow Down / Fear To Tread

48   Chinese Sage / The Shop / Favorite Park

49   GRAMPS

50   Get Busy / Half The World / Silently Roaring

51   Lock The Door / Cammo Up / Autograph

52   Whenever I Can / Forest Dales / Little Giant

53   SPACE AND TIME

54   Strike Zone / Sweet Hookups / Jackpot

55   Fall Steelhead / My Limit / Timeless Technique

56   Rainbow Phantoms / Compassion & Wisdom / Beginning Anew

57   ONE MORE CHANCE

58   Never Dies / If You Can / Plan Of Attack

59   Needle's Eye / Seeking A Wind / Another Miracle

echo

60 Rally Point / For My Head / Best To Come
61 WHEN I GET BACK
62 To The Nines / Waters Never Fished / Willing To Rise
63 Difficult Propositions / Every Ride / Wreckless Abandon
64 Dramatic Scenery / New Objective / More Than Willing
65 GONE FISH'IN
66 This Time / Perpetual Watch / Out Here
67 Cleanup Run / Can Be Found / One Fine Show
68 Find Yourself / Cheap Sunglasses / The Path
69 ANOTHER DAY
70 Painted Red / Along The Way / Hopes And Sins
71 Blink Of An Eye / Ain't Noth'in / Trying To Produce
72 Gonna Go / Four Piece / Good Indication
73 MAKER OF DREAMS
74 Narrow Runs / Drop A Bomb / Duty Required
75 Who Knows / Left Behind / Flag Draped Coffin
76 Ten Thousand Words / Cosmic Rings / Dirty Boots
77 YOU KNOW IT'S TRUE
78 Troubles Behind / Where I've Been / The Key
79 Tested In Action / Get Normal / Well Done
80 Ancient River / Wait My Turn / Heavenly Throne
81 SWEETEST TUNE
82 Soothing Sounds / No One Around / I.E.D.
83 Brighter Than Most / Release The Pain / Heavy Hitter
84 A Little Zen / New Rod / Perfect Forgery
85 MAKE IT SNAPPY
86 Critical Mass / Where I'll Go / Prosthetic Device
87 Perfect Shot / Fly Fishing Fiend / As They Say
88 Inner Peace / Each Morning / Cinch The Straps
89 SECRET ABODE
90 Raw Gust / Little Retreat / Pen And Paper
91 Now And Then / More Than Gold / Unto Yourselves

foxtrot

92   The Mess / Cauldrons Of Fire / As You Know

93   WHISTLES AND BELLS

94   Showing My Bros / Many Trails / Bigger Than Myself

95   One Fine Day / Awareness / Really Need

96   Made It Back / No Stone / Tour Or Two

97   DIG A LITTLE DEEPER

98   The Critics / Mythic Proportion / Trophy

99   Heavy Creels / Red Ropes / Against A Tree

100   Big Sky Country / Stilling My Mind / The Audition

101   DO IT AGAIN

102   Little Sip / Nirvana / Getting Dizzy

103   Cosmic Sea / The Divine / Fear No Evil

104   Put It Away / Come To Life / Cake'n Ice Cream

105   YOU'LL KNOW WHEN

106   Already There / Every Cast / Dazzles My Mind

107   Why Wish / First Step / Things To Come

108   Fully Lived / At My Leisure / My Eyes

109   END OF DAYS

110   Wondering / New Sport / Tighten The Reigns

111   River's Song / Fill My Needs / Time To Relax

112   Test Your Mettle / Bad Intentions / World Class

113   SAVE OUR WORLD

114   Meet Again / Cutthroat Safaris / Closed Mind

115   My Will / Bag Of Tricks / Above And Below

116   Leg And A Drum / Heavy Hand / The Otherside

117   ONLY A TEST

118   More Like Us / Presence Known / It Might Help

119   Polish Your Mirror / Just Dreaming / Welcome Them

120   Any Plate Served / Perceived Change / One Thru Ten

121   PAY ANY PRICE

122   Fast Enough / Magical Key / Gravel Bars

123   Flashes Of Red / Current Seams / Log Jams

golf

124   At Night / Rhythm Of Life / Shake It Off
125   SECRETS OF OLD
126   The Onlookers / On The Natch / Mighty Roar
127   Long Haul / Use It Wisely / Fate Of Nations
128   Stood In Awe / How Much Longer / Thoughtforms
129   THE WINNING TEAM
130   Little Dragon / Ancient Waters / The Hatch
131   Taking Notes / Sharpshooter / How Come
132   Giving Back / Lift Me Up / Next Level
133   OF COURSE
134   Riverdogs / Boulder Strewn Stream / Rainbows Under Water
135   Worth More / Another World / New Life
136   Fluffy Beards / Heavy Burden / Never Forgotten
137   UNIVERSAL SOLDIER
138   Hot L.Z. / Time To Time / Once Again
139   Done Right / Highly Overrated / Shiny Objects
140   No Limit / Watch And Wait / No More
141   BEFORE IT'S GONE
142   Myriad Opportunities / Explode With Laughter / The Illusion
143   Teach The Children Well / Miraculous Events / Middle Way
144   This Far / Price We Paid / Verdant Dimensions
145   ANTICIPATION
146   River Of Life / Clouds In The Sky / On The Line
147   Our Mind / Innuendoes And Impressions / So Sweet
148   Never Change / Place We Go / My Voice
149   OUR OWN DEMISE
150   One Step / As It Appears / In Plain Sight
151   Never Left / Waste No Time / Ultimate Goals
152   Perfect Imposter / The Trail / New Kids
153   THE HUNTER HUNTING
154   No One Knows / Standing Tall / Between The Lines
155   Chug Some Joe / If One Blinked / Perfect Imitation

hotel

156   Never Leave / Swing Of Things / Rivers Of Change
157   NEVER FADE
158   Cosmic Show / I Wonder / City Life
159   Daily Habit / Sweet Music / Slow Current
160   Perpetual Bliss / Every Time / Plain To See
161   MOUNTAIN STORE
162   Blackbird / Raincheck / Favorite Tome
163   Even If / Gonna Trip / Same Clan
164   Dreams And Desires / High On Life / In The Know
165   WIZARD OF CAUSE
166   Future's So Bright / What It Takes / As I Remember
167   Wheel Of Life / Food For Thought / Wishing Well
168   A Cut Above / Wonderful Opportunity / Another Masterpiece
169   LITTLE DECEIVER
170   Road Of Life / Big Picture / Family Bond
171   Every Trick / You Never Know / I Am
172   Green Zone / Covered In Dew / Feed Your Soul
173   SPREAD YOUR WINGS
174   Some Snacks / The Payoff / All One
175   A Few Bros / Future Greatness / Passed Down
176   Platoon Member / Patient Observer / Comforting Glow
177   WATERS
178   Inner Light / Immortality / Idle Chatter
179   All Connected / Let It Go / Counting Blessings
180   Bedtime Story / Sweet Tune / Me And Him
181   SLIPPERY LITTLE FRIENDS
182   2 lb. Test / Click Away / Doggie Bags
183   Cold Brew / Little Chipmunks / Boys From Nam
184   Up Above / Noth'in To It / Common Sense
185   NORTH COUNTRY
186   Week Ahead / Polaroid Film / Plenty To Do
187   Efforless Effort / Us Poets / Pure Energy

188 Hoot Of A Friend / Buckle Down / Impermanence
189 SNEAKY LITTLE DEVIL
190 Same Page / Yoda-Like Action / Old And New
191 Weave Your Web / New Opportunities / Other Tools
192 Light Of Day / Two Thousand Years / Stepping Stones
193 ONE MORE TIME
194 Natural Energy / Selfless Self / Those Who Know
195 See The Truth / All This Time / On The Reel
196 Duty Calls / Morning Routine / Never Ask
197 SECRET WEAPON
198 Cosmic Puzzle / Abide In Awareness / Sitting Still
199 Each Atom / All Phenomena / Like Me
200 Same Cloth / Whatever It Takes / It's Obvious
201 GIANTS OF THE FOREST
202 King's Ransom / Wide Open / Steady Pace
203 Quantum Entanglement / Country Mile / Hidden Dimensions
204 Tomes Of Old / Moon And Stars / Past And Future
205 WAY OF LIFE
206 Brothers In Arms / Those Who Ask / Mountain Majesty
207 Keep The Peace / Ultimate Reality / Mostly Good
208 This Year / Wake Up / Here To Eternity
209 Our Potential / Through The Roof / You Offered
210 Two Legs / Every Detail / Pure Intentions
211 If / Ethereal Warriors / What Really Matters
212 White Robes / Best Laid Plans / Yellow Brick Roads
213 To Be Called / My Mind / Seven Directions
214 Test Of Time / Live And Fight / Warmer Pastures
215 Ancient Race / Never Ending / Creek Freek
216 Move Along / Cosmic Pulse / Seems Like
217 Family Memories / Blue Ship / Perfect Being
218 New Tack / Wise Up / Perpetual Motion
219 What Delights / Make Their Marks / Daily Basis

220   Soothes My Soul / Ebb & Flow / Present Delights
221   Thoughts Of Compassion / Long Strange Trip / Where I Go
222   New Beginning / Will Travel / Prosthetic Devices
223   Our Unit / Under Your Nose / Like I Do
224   Roar And Chirp / More Simple / Last Poem
226   Author's Library Starter Kit List
228   Addendum/Anti-Death Penalty Poems

kilo

FOREWORD

Richard Raugust and I are very fortunate to know one another.

For over 18 years, Richard lived in the Montana State Prison, convicted of a crime he didn't commit. Innocence was not enough to set him free. Richard needed the Montana Innocence Project, and all its staff, volunteers and donors, to finally free him. I am a founder of the Montana Innocence Project.

I am fortunate to know Richard because every time I speak with him, I am struck by his humanity and care for other people. Not surprisingly, Richard's poetry clearly reflects that humanity.

With every right to be bitter and broken, Richard reaches out to people in need. He cares about people who have been treated unfairly by society, as well as those who have seen and experienced events that have left them emotionally crippled. By feeling inward, Richard looks outward. He is unafraid to reveal emotions that could well have been destroyed by his personal history.

Fishers of Trout and Men: Protectors of the Realm is an exercise in contrasts, what is worldly and what is otherworldly. Richard finds connections and connectedness in life and spirit. It is ironic (to say the least) that he lived in an utterly disconnected environment, only to have found associations everywhere. His connections are boundless: they are between people, between heaven and earth, between the spiritual and the historical.

"...(T)hings felt but never seen" are the veterans and fishers alike. Veterans must read these poems to feel the relationship between agony of past trauma and the blissfulness of a beautiful trout on the line. They are not separate; they are deeply correlated. There is elegance and beauty in the struggle and it's okay to be whimsical while you're at it.

Who among us can truly understand that violence will change brain function and alter personality? Indeed, who can believe that universal truth exists with a flick of the wrist and the soft landing of a fly?

Richard's faith informs him and protects him. His spirituality strengthens him. I suppose that, left with little hope and no freedom for so long, a measure of hope and freedom had to appear from somewhere. Being without hope and freedom must be like trying to live without air and water.

I am proud of this man who endured so much for so long; and then, inexplicably by those of us who didn't, he emerged with talents and feelings that others can use and enjoy. This collection of poems honors the struggle of soldiers who occupy a special place in Richard's heart and serves as a testament to Richard's past and his future.

Dan Weinberg, Ph.D.
Retired Montana State Senator
Whitefish, Montana
April, 2016

FISHERS OF TROUT AND MEN

In city dreams
Of rivers near or far,
Tossing and turning
Blinded by unearthly star.
Every color of His rainbow
Holds encounters unbeknownst,
To mortal men guarded
By a heavenly host.
Caught between worlds
Of darkness and light,
We offer good words,
Always fighting the good fight.
From time immemorial
For at least two thousand years,
Those like us as well as
Those of our kind,
Speak few words
And fewer words still speak,
For it is one's destiny then
To lead by example
Being both...
Fishers of trout and men.

HEAVEN'S REWARD
Summer's day
Upon the water
Merely a glimpse
Of heaven's reward

BLOW YOUR MIND
In forest halls
Under azure skies
Awaiting mysteries
That'll blow your mind

FRIENDLY THUD
One more time
Amidst the mist
Calmly anticipating
Another friendly thud

SALT & PEPPER
Through the salad
Without any dressing
Vigorously declining
Table salt and pepper

WHEREVER IT'S FOUND
One more stalk
In unseen realms
Seeking adventure
Wherever it's found

HIDE AND SEEK
Off your couch
And on the crouch
Snell's window playing
Games called hide and seek

PLENTY LEFT
Look'in a little shaggy
But not quite a bum
Two week vacation
With plenty left

IN PUBLIC
On all fours
Though a bit old
I'll crawl to you
Even in public

THINGS BEHIND
At the present moment
Sparklets would be nice
Your shiny little birds
Keep leaving things behind

NEVER SEEN

Working the shoreline
For your next meal,
Looking for movement
In between eddys
Swirling and still.
Shadows moving in
Waters dark and deep,
Just one nice one
One to play and keep.
The ancients must've done it
Something like this,
Working their crude imitations
Hoping for a kiss.
Then out of nowhere
Little fella comes a fly'in,
Shooting for the moon
All game with plenty of try'in.
You've probably been there too
You probably know what I mean,
Cause you're an ancient keeper
Of things felt but never seen.

ANCIENT SAGE
Sorrow with worry
Makes white hair grow
Look into your own mirror
Smiling at the ancient sage

PRESENTATION
You've read all their books
And studied some pictures too
Even got a handful of lessons in
Nuances of the art till you're blue

TEN THOUSAND DOORS
Home with friends and family
My last tour was one wild ride
Angels calling as they fly over
Ten thousand doors are opened wide

BIG BOWS

Up past valleys of death
I've heard of stories sold
Old timers tell their tales
Big bows refusing to be caught

POLISHING MY MIRROR

Calm waters reflecting
Both heaven and skies above
Polishing my mirror of divinity
Stilling our thoughts with wisdom

SOME GOOD

Subtle truths manna falls
Settling on quiet ones below
If we stand still long enough
It'll soak in doing us some good

THE UNDERCUT
Life's really a breeze
Got it made in some shade
No need for cheap sunglasses
Chilling in the undercut

DROP THE FLY
Picture perfect presentations
Once again time after time
Looks quite natural to me
So I drop the fly and then…

TROUT LIES
Calm pools sans disturbance
Facing upstream in the wind
Sails filled to overflowing
Trout lies with your friends

WHAT CAN YOU DO?

In crystal pools
From mountain's peak,
Weaving and bobbing
For food we thus speak.
Our way of life
Is a lot like yours,
Swimming through our dimension
While you prefer doors.
There's really not much difference
In how we exist,
Both of us seek happiness
But we have the shorter list:
Food, shelter, freedom to roam
Wondering and wandering
From home to home.
If we'd all pull together
As a team with one another,
Perhaps we could use our heads
Doing more than dream, my brother.
Often having more than we need
While many more have not,
It isn't as hard as it seems
If you'd use a little thought.
Action – is what we want,
No go out and show us
What you can do.

PRIME RUN
Cruising the boulevard
On any saturday night
You can usually find me
In our local prime run

GLASSY WATER
Not a cloud in sight
Nor a breeze to buffet
No undulations to fight
Glassy water surrounds

INNER LIFE
Few people take the time
To make their greatest trip
A journey of countless lifetimes
Begins on roads to your inner life

BLUE PLANET
Rivers rambling to the sea
Flaxen strands of golden fleece
Eyes glimmering in night's parade
This blue planet making her rounds

PROUD TO BE
Sands of time march on
And bells toll for thee
Behind clouds moon peeks
Be proud to be who you be

SOMETHING TO GRASP
Nothing's permanent
In rivers of change
I'm seeking the Holy
For something to grasp

CONSTANT CHANGE

Appearances can confound
At first glance appear reel
Empty of inherent existence
Constant change is my friend

FAVORITE STREAM

Flocks of birds chatter
Singing His favorite tune
Wind's tickling our fancies
My favorite stream wins again

ABOUT TO BEGIN

Afternoon delights
Start to fade away
Trips back to camp
Are about to begin

AS IT STANDS NOW

Day's life dawns
Amid alpine meadows,
With babbling brooks
Dancing for all below.
It's times like these
Worth infinitely more
Than the price we pay
For your weekend excursions.
Mountains surely hold
Magical mystery tours,
With keepers of heaven
Watching all who know.
From time long gone
Perhaps millions of years,
An ancient race
To this present day.
Now we ask you all
To do more than your part,
As it stands now
Your heads make
Mighty fine hat racks.

DAILY ROUNDS
Bluejays and flowers and more
Are none too rare to notice
Nor bees' n hoppers or bugs
Making their daily rounds

TROUBLED MINDS
Chasing memories gone long
Of faded battles gone by
Ripples in the currents
Soothes troubled minds

NOTHING TO COMPARE
Pristine beauty
Around me abounding
Scent of forest's waft
With nothing to compare

RETURNING HOME
Spring winds growing
Giants dance around me
I'll go where it blows
Always returning home

IN REMEMBRANCE
Entering gates at dawn
New adventures beckoning
Casting some shots for us
In remembrance of our past

TRYING TO MAKE SENSE
Another year walks
Awaiting your arrival
I feel you're watch'in me
Try to make sense of it all

YOUR LIFE

Tossing a few coins into
Water where woods run deep
It's a small token to be sure
That mission paid with your life

TAKE YOUR SEATS

Raising the baton
As symphony surrounds
Creating masterpieces
Please take your seats

LITTLE CASTLE

Everyone has theirs
Some rarer than others
Using the shade and cover
A little castle in your woods

MAKE THE RIGHT DECISION

Forty days into
Trials beyond belief,
Mara and evil spectres
With thirst beyond relief.
The test of a lifetime
To see if I had any juice,
Was I merely a seeker
One to do or die or dare,
Or was I really a keeper
Of things from beyond'n rare?
This potential we thus hold
Burried deep within our soul,
Sometimes hard to fathom
Gifts from ancients of old.
Your destiny's been laid out
For you to find and sow,
We watch you on a daily basis
Search and seek and grow.
Now that we understand
You're really on a mission,
Go out leading by example
Always making right decisions.

FEED LANE

Into nature's aisle
With 10 items or less
I'm certainly in no hurry
Perusing the feed lane we go

DECEPTION AND GUILE

Wearing wild-assed gear
Gussied up over the wazoo
One more secret rendevouz
Using deception and guile

REELY SCREAM

With none to share our spread
Cheese, crackers and whine
Line stinging my fingers
You reely scream good

ANOTHER TOUR
Mountain roads rambling
Spotter riding shotgun
Starting to look like
I'm on another tour

INNER EYE
Subtle winds whisper
Tickling our inner ear
Trying to open doorways
Seeking with my inner eye

RIVER CALLS
Cities of gold'n silver
Food for our head awaits
From way up high falling
River's calling you home

YELLOW MOON
Me and my thoughts alone
Deep within quietness abides
Sitting amongst laden hilltops
Until the yellow moon comes alive

THE PUZZLE
Answering your call
Doing what's required
Opening intricate boxes
Trying to put it together

REALMS UNKNOWN
Where are we from friend
Mortals of elemental fire
Perhaps we're not from here
Tis why we seek realms unknown

FORT BENNING

Working another field
Life F.O.'s in-country,
You'd better not stir
Or your jig'll be up.
See I've been to the fort
Tried, tested and true,
We love to ruck and fight
Wetting our line too.
We did dirty jobs
That few could endure,
Some of us made it back
Now we hunt trout as a cure.
So if you see us in the bush
Don't make any sudden move,
Some of us are still a bit quick
To react unkindly out of the blue.
Just give us a wave
And if your favor's returned,
We might give you a shout
So you can come on over
And ask us what about...???

LUCKIEST SOUL
A fine summer's day upon my favorite jewel
Dragonflys and bumblebees buzzing me a tune
Riverbirds and butterflys perform at random
When realizing I'm the luckiest soul alive

FORGIVEN
On warm tranquil nights
City lights seem to confound
I knew it was gonna happen again
Asking one more time I am comforted

BE WHO YOU ARE
Beginnings of fall when colors show
Life's cycle is plain for all to see
Take time to appreciate everyday moments
Be who you are not what the status quo says

LITTLE BOOK

Paying with gifts of life
Noble men in uncommon dress
Certainly you've entered into
God's favorite little black book

SPORT AND ADVENTURE

Having yielded my post
To the next soldier on duty
I can't seem to shake it off
Thirsting for sport and adventure

NEXT FORMATION

Western skies tend to soothe
Where sun rests his weary head
Brothers in arms still holding
Waiting for the next formation

PATIENCE AND WISDOM
This road of life holds
Many obstacles to defeat
Paths of least resistance
Takes patience and wisdom

GRAPHITE WHIP
Wind, sands and sun
I've traded it all in
Working a new green zone
With graphite whips for guns

THE WAY
Dragon's breath settling low
Shrouding my favorite hole
Thinking I'll enter into
He and I one in the way

SECRET HOLE

Over some hills
Through thin dales,
Two miles into
Trails rarely trod,
Your secret hole awaits.
Its mythical status
Is whispered about
In coffee shops
And hardware stores,
Tourists only catch
A hint of it
Here or there.
No – this (spot)
Is for locals only.
Some have said
When you arrive
If lady luck
Has been vigilant,
You may sense a glimpse
Of the other side.

FISHER OF MEN
Leave chance and desire behind
Flowing with your cosmic wind
Among all our other leaders
I prefer the fisher of men

ANOTHER SHOT
Winter winds roll and stroll
Into valleys biting my face
Pulling the wool tighter
Shooting another shot

VIGOR AND LIFE
Wherever darkness is found
A lone traveller travels
Through distant galaxies
Casting vigor and life

THINGS TO COME
Falling pinecones dance
Summer closes his door
Autumn's breath calling
Hinting at things to come

SEEK AND ROAM
Deserted campfires die
City dwellers heading home
Best time to pack it up
Best time to seek and roam

EYE TO EYE
Patiently waiting in the cut
For offers bright and true
If you work's just right
We might see eye to eye

MY DREAMS
Many moons ago
Stories once read
I'm finally on the page
North country of my dreams

PERFECT SHOW
Life's certainly a tour
In animated dramatization
Better change your channel
And create the perfect show

TO BE DESIRED
Day's light fades fast
Me and my memories relax
The ancient road to peace
Leaves a lot to be desired

IT COULD BE HAD

Eternal truths in
Winds swirl round,
This daily grind
Keeps us doubting
Hoping to be found.
Next door neighbors
Right across our street
Seem like worlds away,
Must we continually avoid them
Like there's nothing else to do?
We're a nation of one
A world of many,
When are we going to
Share what we've got
Opening our hearts with plenty?
We have the capability
It's in our human nature,
So why don't we all wise up
And feed and care and nurture?
Let's put all wars away
Bringing everyone along;
It could be had for a penny,
A sixpence, a euro, a yaun,
A dollar, a pound, a franc and yen,
A rupee, a peso, a deutsche mark,
A lira, a sheqel, a dinar,
A ruble, a riyal and a won,
A krona, a dirham, a bolivar,
A krone, a prayer and a song.

NOW GONE
The heavy toll of a hot L.Z.
Friends and brothers in arms
Red sunset on laughing waves
Each one here but now gone

TAME AND CONQUER
Rising and falling
Of grief or despair
Only one more enemy
To tame and conquer

WARMED UP
Following the royal paths
Takes patience and effort
Thirty mile ruck marches
Just got me warmed up

HAD TO BE DONE
Views from where we stand
Often clouded with doubt
Fog still mists my eyes
But it had to be done

HEAVEN'S DOOR
Above the timberline
In glacial's cold melt
Alpine lakes and meadows
Knocking on heaven's door

RIDE THE CURRENTS
Carried in His arms
The north winds flow
Birds riding currents
Honking at casters below

WHILE I DANCE
The tides ebb and flow
West winds blow then die
Sun and moon rise and fall
As I dance between them all

STIR THE FIRE
8,000 ft. twin lakes lay
Anticipating morning's rise
0:200 yellow moon's so bright
I stir the fire under night's sun

MISSION'S DONE
Flat as a pancake
Slithering like a snake
No trick's spared
Until the mission's done

COSMIC EMBRACE

You giver of life
You washer awayer of sins,
You fall from heaven's abode
Nourishing Innefable's little kids.
With facets too vast to enumerate
Like manna from invisible realms,
We play and grow in gifts to us all
Between summer and winter, spring or fall.
There are those of us who likely
Hold a special place in your heart,
Primordial states of your beginninglessness
Fishers who emanate from your thought.
Some say we wear funny hats
And vests with lots of pockets too,
While also seeking and searching
Your hidden dimensions.
We rise up early
Before your bringer of life
Makes his presence known,
Often…before bluebirds have flown.
We raise up our little ones
Washing dreamtime from their face,
Then we don our weapons of war
Stalking slippery rainbows
Under the vastness of
Your cosmic embrace.

LONG WHITE ROBES
Waters of life wells from within
And heaven's kingdom is always nearby
With dedicated effort to save the planet
You represent ancients in long white robes

WITH NARY A CARE
Driven by desires from who knows where
Thoughts and actions that have basis none
Invisible forces push and pull without rest
Immortals acting like rookies with nary a care

NOTHING BUT
Once separated ore from gold
After the dust finally settles
Taking away preconceived notions
Nothing but another miracle to view

AIN'T EASY

One more year's on the blow
Wondering if I've done enough
In this web of life a daily show
Keep'in up with my mind ain't easy

WHITE CRANE

Death or glory in zones of fire
Ten thousand years stillness reigns
White cranes stand at attention
Holding their heads in shame

MAKING NOISE

Engines of war continually roar
Spectators watch bells jingle
Like steeds on a dress march
Making noise simulating war

FROM THE CAPITOL
Years of service standing tall
Action distilled in fogs of war
Smoke and powder burning my eyes
How can they see from the capitol

STRAIGHT AND NARROW
Serving forces from afar
Soldiers in pressed camouflage
Bright medallions and silver stars
Please lead us to the straight and narrow

DOPE I PREFER
Looking for the medicine
To ease troubled minds
Going to purer waters
Is the dope I prefer

STEWARDS OF THE PLANET

I come to greet you
On bygone battlegrounds,
Where earth and sky
Meet near world's edge.
You roam and wander
In antediluvian dimensions,
Waiting for supernatural delights
Wafting their wayward way
To locations dear to you.
You're a simple creature
Slipping and sliding
In cool wetness,
Making it look easy.
You've been around
For millions of years,
Though we don't help much
Polluting your ancient and sacred ways.
I apologize for our ignorance,
Although it doesn't do you much good
When you're all choked up coughing
Because us stewards of the planet
Just don't get it.

NEVER SAYING NO
Dancing your pants off
Flashes, swirls and bumps
This whole world's my stage
Little friends never saying no

CHECK THE FRIDGE
Artificial presentations
But you must be on a diet
I've thrown the sink at you
Now I'm off to check my fridge

MY BUDDIES
Sporting a vest with no plates
Our freedom of movement
Comes at a fine price
My buddies already paid the tab

SPLITTING JOKES
Burning the midnight oil
In our shop that never sleeps
Me and those who've made it back
Splitting jokes and bamboo for fun

WHERE I GO
Water ejects off outstretched line
Invisible forces from under dine
Where I go from time to time
To bring the balance back

NO CLAIM
Climbing over the top
On this spiritual quest
Impossible to slow me down
Worry and doubt have no claim

ANCIENT DOMAIN
Creatures of the forest
Roaming and rambling along
I've seen them now and then
Entering their ancient domain

CLINGING
Days'n years come to pass
Like clouds in a clear sky
So I've released all clinging
Trying to bring my friends along

START AGAIN
Sometimes grief seems to consume
And the best laid plans
Get F.U.B.A.R.
Then I regroup and start again

SAME OLD STORY

One more hot LZ
Another hot'n deadly landing,
To our first and last man standing.
We heard the oppressed's call,
We heard your people calling,
Now we stand at attention
Ready or not with no stalling.
This job's not real pretty
Nor are sights'n sounds of war,
Who knows if peace is winning
Who really knows the score?
All we can do is train
Lifting up our fellow man,
If oppressed they be
In whatever shape, color or land.
It will sure be nice
When world leaders no more
Fight for ego, boundry or glory,
After several thousand years
You'd think they'd wake up
Instead of still praising
The same old story.

PAY US BACK
Raising our cover
For red white and blue
Who knows the price we paid
Is anybody going to pay us back

SOON ENOUGH
Your actions are all your own
No one else knows what they mean
Carry on always leading by example
They will figure it out soon enough

LITTLE FINGER
When anxiety floats about
Pots and pans get tossed
Bending our pinky finger
My own nuclear reactor

MEMORIES
Leaning against giant soldiers
Sampling smoked trout'n cheese
I tip one to quench my thirst
Savoring memories gone by

I'M LUCKY
Pages adorning the wall
Fall like snowflakes fading
Millennia to come and gone
I'm lucky to be alive

TESTED AND TRUE
Rising to any occasion
Cause that's what we do
Naturally in our natures
Been tried, tested and true

S.A.W.

With a heave and a ho
The loop recoils back
Quite a bit quieter
Than the bolt on my s.a.w.

DIMPLE HER WATER

Temples in forests
Rainbows rise to feed
Please tip your waitress
After you dimple her water

FAT LIPS

You have it all staked out
The whole hole's been claimed
I guess you've earned it though
With enough fat lips to prove it

GO TO THE WATER

Hustles'n bustles
Of nine to fives,
Forty plus a week
Oftentimes more,
Just to stay alive.
Friends, families
Appointments galore,
No time to rest or
Catch your breath,
No time to go inside
And build your inner store.
Our outside world
Keeps most dazed or confused
Mental battles on a daily basis
Leaves us cold, tired, wet, and abused.
There's more to this life
Than meets mortal eyes,
If you slow down long enough
There'll be no need wondering why.
These material worlds
Are not what really matters,
That's why it's so important
To stop all your internal chatter.
Step away from plastic remotes
Getting out into nature,
It'll give you time to reflect
(We can help you do it)
If you make up your mind
And go to the water.

DUET

We have style'n grace aplenty
While performing our duet
Using dead-drift numbers
Always knock'em dead

NEXT MOVE

Have brass in pocket
A little time to kill
Breaking out the topo
Plotting my next move

MORE OFTEN

Undulations perpetually shimmer
Rippling the fabric of space
Vibrations tickle my senses
Need to do it more often

LONG THROW

Not your local hangout
A double and fries to go
It'll surely be fulfilling
The slurp after a long throw

SLOW DOWN

We all have our fair share
Diamonds in roughness galore
If you slow down a minute or two
They usually bubble to the surface

FEAR TO TREAD

11B, airborne rangers
You got your wings
And play in fires
Where mortals fear to tread

CHINESE SAGE

Sitting on banks stilling
Memories flotsam and jetsam
Down rivers of time enjoying
Chilling like a Chinese sage

THE SHOP

Winter's grip is thawing
When things become all new
Activity explodes everywhere
Better hustle back to the shop

FAVORITE PARK

Grand palace mountains be
Golden gates greeting guests
Distant clouds soften and glow
My favorite park welcomes us back

GRAMPS

Zero 4:30 as he comes creeping upon the floor,
(rise and shine sunshine,
It's time to wet our line –
2 bits – 2 bits – 2 bits) as we bet,
Settling on day's potential score.
Pancakes from scratch,
Coffee's on the boil,
Sandwiches, cookies'n chips for road's trip
Thermos topped off as we lock shop's door.
Hidden streams, rivers, creeks, and lakes,
His motto was get your job done whatever it takes.
We're off to spots where mortals rarely tread...
One more visit with mother nature,
Bringing me up under her watchful eye
Growing like a weed springing to mature.
At trail's head we check our list twice,
Trips back to our van are signs of a novice
And I'm three years into this ancient brotherhood,
Nearly a journeyman by most accounts.
Hooks, swivels, bb shot, 2 lb. test with 4 lb. line,
Certainly a young man's treasure chest
Who could have asked for more?

GET BUSY

Sending my wishes out
For a long life for thee
So much I haven't seen yet
Better roger up and get busy

HALF THE WORLD

Following thoughts
Over midnight's dreams
How far can I expect to go
Already covered half the world

SILENTLY ROARING

Bright moon skating
Across rivers of stars
Sitting back I'm pondering
Silently roaring with applause

LOCK THE DOOR
My country estate
In downtown dwells
Mount Shasta beckons
Better lock the doors

CAMMO UP
In bags of maps and gear
I hear special tools calling
They chant'n hum royal orders
Better cammo up and grab my rod

AUTOGRAPH
Sharing events hard to fathom
Composing poems to soothe souls
If my english teacher saw me now
She'd probably ask for an autograph

WHENEVER I CAN

Where rivers run dark and deep
And giants stand for all to see
Heading into remote destinations
City for wilderness whenever I can

FOREST DALES

Old yeller was always willing
Never been a road dog more faithful
Now one of his kids and myself
Stalk yellow belly in hidden glens

LITTLE GIANT

You've got a nice outfit
A little brighter than most
Some say you're too small though
Little giants sporting speckled skin

SPACE AND TIME

They say you're a foe
With sport to spare,
In streams and brooks
From pole to pole.
Some call you
Phantom of the river,
Wherever you roam
Any name given
Is elusive as your self.
While you slip'n slide
In your watery world,
We plot then stalk you
Like generals afield.
Shooting our shot
Under bank or rock,
Using Sun Tzu's tactics
We're certainly undergunned.
Rising before reveille
When time we can find
Allows us to hook up,
One little joy left over
Floating with you and your kind
Through this cosmic river
Of space and time.

STRIKE ZONE
Trading in my day job
In foreign lands have trod
Shooting for that perfect hole
Strike zones without return fire

SWEET HOOKUPS
Tossing and casting into
A postcard-shot to remember
Hoping you've got the connect
I've always liked sweet hookups

JACKPOT
Swinging to and fro
Me, my boys and bros
It's a safe bet to bet
Always a jackpot in store

FALL STEELHEAD
Autumn leaves brighten
Dancing on invisible breeze
Thermometer beginning to drop
Must be time for fall steelhead

MY LIMIT
Wading for action
Under rising sun
Lunch can wait
Till my limit's caught

TIMELESS TECHNIQUE
Between 10:00 and 2:00
Or perhaps 9:00 and 3:00
Steady hands hold and sway
Timeless technique wins again

RAINBOW PHANTOMS
Been in piles of heavy shit
At least a couple dozen times
Now I'd prefer waist deep water
Hunting rainbow phantoms sublime

COMPASSION AND WISDOM
Plato certainly spoke about them
Philosopher-kings ruling the lands
I'll take combat soldiers every time
Steeped in fire, compassion and wisdom

BEGINNING ANEW
Ominous clouds say warning
The soldier takes a first step
Ten thousand mile journeys begin
Parting with old ways beginning anew

ONE MORE CHANCE

Casting our flies
Like merlin on rout,
Conducting the orchestra
Without ever a doubt.
From times long gone
From memories faded past,
It's this ancient tradition
In rivers calm and fast.
We bring our magic
To waters never seen,
On mountainsides so frail
And forest dales so green.
Those of us who know of
Invisible realms divine,
Seek His kingdom to come
And one more chance
To wet our line.

NEVER DIES

Places buried deep within
Processes of farewell begins
Never the easiest thing to do
An old friend's memory never dies

IF YOU CAN

Ups and downs of life you'll find
Surely more common than wind and rain
It's the greatest challenge of our cosmos
To prevail if you can or accept if you must

PLAN OF ATTACK

Obstacles often confront
Wary wayfarers on their way
Find yourself in aromatic abodes
And figure out your plan of attack

NEEDLE'S EYE

My path follows mountains seen
With roads both long and narrow
Through valleys of life and death
As my horse seeks the needle's eye

SEEKING A WIND

Our midnight sun rises faithfully
On her journey that knows no end
And every morning I do the same
Seeking a wind to puff my sail

ANOTHER MIRACLE

Back from the chaos
A country came calling
I witness another miracle
When my limbs touch the floor

RALLY POINT

Quiet places in woods I see
Slices of heaven in forests be
Think I'll build our retreat here
A rally point for my bros to gather

FOR MY HEAD

When flows gently grow
Big pools seem to contain
Little monsters with red bands
And other treasures for my head

BEST TO COME

On my favorite stretch
With holes known by heart
Saving our favorite for last
Like life with the best to come

WHEN I GET BACK

Sun-scorched souls
Sand stings my face,
81 and a wake up
Maybe I'll get out of this place?
Said they need me back
I'm on my second tour,
Couldn't let my boys down
Hummer's fueled ready for war.
It's one helluva ride
Through valleys dodging death,
Let's not forget sniper's alley:
Better hold your breath!
It's such a shame that
It comes down to this,
Death and destruction
With very little bliss.
Looking to our futures
Potential greener grass,
Gonna stand up to end war
Ain't gonna give it a pass.
When I get stateside
I'm gonna get into;
Social justice and
Organic gardening,
Family time and
Fly fishing,
Motorcycle riding and
Making a difference
While I dig my head.

TO THE NINES
Boarding another big bird
Rucks're loaded to the nines
Here I come far flung corners
This time hunt'in trout instead

WATERS NEVER FISHED
Wild rides stateside
Into waters never fished
This is starting to excite me
No need to dodge flying tablets

WILLING TO RISE
Early morning routine
Stoking breakfast fires
Are you as willing to rise
As one such as myself

DIFFICULT PROPOSITIONS
Decisions, decisions, decisions
Where are we gonna head to this year
I hear there are hidden places in Montana
Difficult propositions with nothing to lose

EVERY RIDE
High plains drifter
Tramp fisherman and more
Like floating nymphs cruising
Every ride better than the last

WRECKLESS ABANDON
Got a high pitched squeal
You're my newest favorite sound
Doing it again with wreckless abandon
I'll give you 100 yds. and not an inch more

DRAMATIC SCENERY

Super high action drama
Lots of red'n gory trauma
Now I'm blowing my mind with
New kinds of dramatic scenery

NEW OBJECTIVE

Remote valleys and ridges
Theoretically not on patrol
Working more rugged landscape
With a healthier new objective

MORE THAN WILLING

Another day comes to life
With potential beyond belief
Always been up before reveille
I've always been more than willing

GONE FISH'IN

Fly'in through currents
Without any wings,
Line's haul'in ass
As old orvis really sings.
Another day upon waters
Sharing moments that last,
Me, my boy and daughters.
Up before sun's early rise
Underneath ancient watchers
Golden rays with violet skies,
Wondering if heaven...
Is as good as this?
It's times like these
With family and friends you know
That makes all this nonsense
Just another walk in His park.
So if you've yet to try it
Saddle up the little ones
Giving your boss a report:
GONE FISH'IN!

THIS TIME
One more lonely reception
From combat zones far afield
My brothers from nam were dissed
Please try and do better this time

PERPETUAL WATCH
Creatures of the realm
Chirp and chatter all day
Another calm restful night
With stars on perpetual watch

OUT HERE
Moon shines brighter near the peak
Lone fishers plying their trade
City life is okay for a few
Out here souls eat well

CLEANUP RUN

Sealed orders from stars come
Radio traffic beginning to boil
Birds come chop chirp choppin in
Get ready for another cleanup run

CAN BE FOUND

Red sun rising grows
Warming one's inner life
Roads to heaven can be found
Mindfully breathing in and out

ONE FINE SHOW

White whisps form before our eyes
Breezes are beginning to speak
Tree tops start their thing
Putting on one fine show

FIND YOURSELF
Travelling hand in hand
To ultimate goals going
Find yourself a partner
To smooth out the bumps

CHEAP SUNGLASSES
Climbing stairways to heaven
Or whatever path you may seek
Better don some cheap sunglasses
Future's brighter than you thought

THE PATH
If only I'd known about
Yellow brick roads back then
Perhaps I'd have taken a right
And chosen the path less followed

ANOTHER DAY

I see you there
Standing on banks,
Dressed to kill and
Loaded for bear.
You're all geared up
For a momentous event,
I can see you clearly
But rarely can you see me.
We watch you move
Upon and over rocks,
Sometimes narrowly
Escaping death.
The lengths you all go
To share a few moments
Of our precious time,
Never ceases to amaze us.
We applaud your efforts,
Though we appreciate it most
When you let us go to
Live and fight
Another day.

PAINTED RED

Visiting friends at the wall
A gathering place set in stones
Looking up at these white buildings
Wondering how they'd feel painted red

ALONG THE WAY

Most of us dwell on past events
Tending to foster hurtful events
Now I'm creating a brighter future
Counting my blessings along the way

HOPES AND SINS

Walls guarding realms divine
Through crystal halls I roamed
A certified vagabond in the winds
Between life and death, hopes'n sins

BLINK OF AN EYE
In hollows past and present
Separated by thin cosmic skies
Then and now soldiers of fortune
Life lived in the blink of an eye

AIN'T NOTH'IN
Chip, chip, chip'in away
On the path climbing higher
Sometimes roads get a bit hairy
It ain't noth'in for a guy like me

TRYING TO PRODUCE
Working magical mojo
Like there's not to lose
Rabbits jump in funny hats
While trying to produce a rise

GONNA GO

Off in the distance
Cold winds come blowing
Rain, sun, sleet or shine
Gonna go even if it's snowing

FOUR PIECE

My honey wants a new furniture set again
Said old one's way past worn out and has been
I can afford a two thigh/breasts chicken dinner
But the four piece fly rod has already been ordered

GOOD INDICATION

Tapping my fingers and racking my brains
The fact that you've just read this little poem
Is a good indication and affirmatively establishes
A miracle has just occurred right before your very eyes

MAKER OF DREAMS

As you popped up
To kiss the sky,
Tasting tasty morsels
Caught in your watchful eye,
I thought of trips past
With my son in tow,
Memories remembered
In campfires long ago,
Still glimmering sparks
Through corners of my mind.
Counting these times
A futile endeavor,
Certainly more than
I care to ponder.
So thank you – my little
Maker of dreams,
Time to grab our gear
And show the boy
How we dance.

NARROW RUNS

Wide rivers roaring softly
Between peaks carved in stone
Where I seek infinite rainbows
Are narrow runs in fields of gold

DROP A BOMB

Waiting below riffles
Ready to snatch a snack
Casting beyond snell's window
Gonna drop a bomb on you this time

DUTY REQUIRED

In your tireless service naturally
A country puts her best foot forward
United efforts denying tyrants at large
Where you often did more than duty required

WHO KNOWS
In distant campaigns
Across foreign domains
Columns of soldiers depart
Who knows how many'll return

LEFT BEHIND
Conductors gave the signal
For drums and brass to begin
Another battalion's off-loading
Hoping their demons were left behind

FLAG DRAPED COFFIN
Palettes of colors adorns your chest
You're all spiffied up in your pressed
Boots sparkle in the formation as well
Hard to salute in a flag draped coffin

TEN THOUSAND WORDS

Another battle set in pen
Blue blood drips from his men
Actions worth ten thousand words
Will someone please change the script

COSMIC RINGS

Warrior's code for eons stands
An eternal truth set in stone
Mortals play in cosmic rings
The games of immortal kings

DIRTY BOOTS

Transcending this bag of bones
Our lotus in mud does surely grow
Beauty that never has end or compare
With dirty boots and an immaculate soul

YOU KNOW IT'S TRUE

Our weekend games
In this leisure world,
With trips on planes
Another nation's consumed.
It's times like these
When apathy abounds,
The pale horse gallops
Making his daily rounds.
News media today
With powers that be,
Feed us what they want
Keeping us blind
And not so free.
One of these days
We'd better wake up,
New leaders among us
Wise, wary and uncorrupt.
It's a sad situation
When to err on caution's side
Is just a novel saying from our past,
Because deep down we all know it's true!
So do your part please
Starting or joining today
If we're ever going to make it
We must unite and think and pray!

TROUBLES BEHIND

Getting accustomed to civilian life
Hugging and kissing my beautiful wife
Time to get back into the swing of things
Way past time to leave our troubles behind

WHERE I'VE BEEN

In through the out door
Going out through the in
Sitting with sifu meditating
Trying to grasp where I've been

THE KEY

On a journey that begins with a step
Starting perhaps before big bangs began
This cosmic consciousness no end in sight
If only I'd remember where I put those keys

TESTED IN ACTION

Our minds are full of worry and doubt
With constant pressure to always succeed
You've been tested in action once or twice
How much more assurance does an employer need

GET NORMAL

Old friends from combat meet
Not quite as often as they should
Life begins to get normal once more
Better slow down and count your blessings

WELL DONE

Feeling like ancient prodigal sons
Knowing full well a mission well done
Now you're back though feeling a bit blue
Pat yourself on the back if no one else will

ANCIENT RIVER

You're an inspiration to more than you know
Hard suppressing memories that often trouble
Doubts'n innuendoes that surface or bubble
Flowing like an ancient river you press on

WAIT MY TURN

Heavenly steps are built and have been
Waiting for patrons to begin to arrive
Some of your bros are making their way
Think I'll slow down and wait my turn

HEAVENLY THRONE

Drugs and alcohol unfortunately suppress
Innate clarity and insight below the surface
When leaving bad habits behind to whither alone
A seat at the top awaiting is your heavenly throne

SWEETEST TUNE

You're a representative
Of Indivisible's truths,
Occasionally hard to fathom though
Because you need a little proof.
Our ultimate reality
Is unlimited ascension,
You're His eyes, ears and voice
In this limited dimension.
It's really no big deal
If you care to cope,
With the Creator's creation
Filled to overflowing
With love and hope.
Most of us forget
Mysteries that we hold,
Written in countless pages
How many times need you be told?
Willpower in superconsciousness
Does shape reality more,
Going back billions of years
Is the heart of our celestial core.
His soul of creation
Be not organic made,
In this life driven cosmos
Being the sweetest tune
Forever played.

SOOTHING SOUNDS
Ringing in my ears or ptsd
Never seeming to go on leave
Look for me heading into the hills
Where I crank up subtle soothing sounds

NO ONE AROUND
Tickling the surface like a skilled surgeon
We danced around your most likely spots
Doing our thing we dapped some more
Not noticing no one was around

I.E.D.
Delicately selecting every single step
Floating line caressing surface tension
Finessing your way into perfect position
Boom! Bam! Gotcha!!! his famous last words

BRIGHTER THAN MOST
She's a real doll ready to impress
Always eager to dance and give her best
She's a little brighter than most others
To dollies in the cut I raise a toast

RELEASE THE PAIN
At the drop of a hat or moment's notice
36-hour readiness unit ready to rock'n roll
Now that we've done it with style and aplomb
Gonna drop down a few gears and release the pain

HEAVY HITTER
You're a real tough cookie bro
A battle buddy never been a doubt
A heavy hitter topping every list
Now we've got to try and act normal

A LITTLE ZEN
Waiting for some nibbles
Or just another tug on my line
This suspense is killing me softly
Super focused and feeling a little zen

NEW ROD
Standing behind surface to airs
Probably not the wisest thing to do
Nor would you fare well in my blast area
This is a new rod and I'm just a bit rusty

PERFECT FORGERY
You've got your credentials
Licensed up'n stamped for sure
Now you open your tiny tin house
Searching for that perfect forgery

MAKE IT SNAPPY

Sun's arrows
Soak canyon walls,
With river's roar
Stilling time.
Life's but a dream
Although it feels
Harder than it seems,
So I come here often
To reaffirm the spell.
Molecules of matter
Spinning out of orbit,
A new phenomenon
Is about to begin.
Mad as a hatter
Dodging daily disaster,
It might be time to
Pull together as a team.
If you're on our bus
Get off their fence,
Of course actions speak
Louder than words,
Now go shape reality
And make it snappy!

CRITICAL MASS
Another faint whisper heard
From a fish that makes no noise
Sounds that're real hard to decipher
Till the murmur's reached critical mass

WHERE I'LL GO
Overhead cover is nice in a hot L.Z.
Now that I'm back it's not required
For some reason you sure love it
It's where I'll go to find you

PROSTHETIC DEVICE
Smoother evener strokes casting
Like you've done it a million times
Working your magic like Merlin on stage
With your prosthetic device defying all odds

PERFECT SHOT
With little to no wind
The day's gonna be special
Waiting to punch your first hole
Trying to make another perfect shot

FLY FISHING FIEND
After six months of rehab
Leaving your crutches behind
A walking stick now rides shotgun
What's a fly fishing fiend gonna do

AS THEY SAY
Following's okay in a draft
Saving fuel for the final sprint
But you're a fisher of trout and men
As they say proof's in the pudding

INNER PEACE

Dazzling lights in bigger cities thrilled
Kind of boring if you've been over there
Now I seek finding my inner peace where
The fins'n the foul always find theirs

EACH MORNING

On solitary shores heading to the next
Humble men seek in this sea of life
We wake up each morning hoping to
Help more than the day before

CINCH THE STRAPS

Climbing towers like Jacob of old
Between heaven and earth in the rift
A journey that has to be done sometime
Cinching the straps take your next step

SECRET ABODE

Early morning smoke
Crackles on breakfast's fire,
Forest's fresh fragrance
Fills my senses full.
Another primordial setting
With intuition as my guide,
I'm off to do the impossible…
I'm off to prove you're alive.
No one has seen you
For some sixty odd years,
But I sense you're out there
Waiting to sip my fly.
I've had this hunch
Your secret abode,
It's a place where elders go
When remembering days gone by.
I realize it's a long way out
Into country heard about
But rarely seen,
Should be no problem for me
As I've done a tour through hell
And need to clear my head.

RAW GUST

When leaves of autumn start to depart'n fly
A raw gust shimmers with purple and gold
This timeless picture has been scriven
More Kodak moments without any film

LITTLE RETREAT

Our road of life never ends
The rally point is way on high
I built this little retreat here
Where me and my bros can practice

PEN AND PAPER

Missions bubble in cavern's keep
Words hardly ever do them justice
So I pick up pen and paper writing
Hoping others'll learn from our past

NOW AND THEN
Brothers in arms now and then
Stories relived never forgotten
Loitering around campfire's glow
When will we be needed no more

MORE THAN GOLD
O ye guardians of delicate balance
Between time's and eternity's space
The price you pay to keep our faith
White feathers worth more than gold

UNTO YOURSELVES
Paths of peace are hard to find
Walk away from fortune and fame
Build your temple pay any price
Be ye lamps unto yourselves

THE MESS
You cooked it off just right
Like some old jiffy-pop snacks
One problem you might not know
The mess is harder to clean up

CAULDRONS OF FIRE
You've weathered storms more than most
Between life and death with the Holy Ghost
It's times like these worth more than others
Through cauldrons of fires with your brothers

AS YOU KNOW
Rally up the troops
Lacing up your two boots
Live like there's no tomorrow
As you know there might not be

WHISTLES AND BELLS

Checking my tackle
For magic of choice,
Listening for insights
From His mystical voice.
Spinners and spells,
Whistles and bells,
I was about to perform
On world's stage.
Audiences were waiting
To see what I brought,
Would I make'm laugh
Without ever a thought,
Or would I dazzle'm all
Between green and gold,
Crimson or gray?
It was up to me,
It was I make the call.
From coast to coast
And over any sea,
It was me or him
Him or me.

SHOWING MY BROS
Clinging to no thing
Polishing my mirror within
Guardian of serenity standing
Showing my bros how to get'er done

MANY TRAILS
Lamps of wisdom yearning
Lighting our inner journeys
There are many trails to follow
So pick one and take the first step

BIGGER THAN MYSELF
Failing to leave forests by dark
Shadows of other worlds growing
Teasing my mind into awareness
Of things bigger than myself

ONE FINE DAY
Robes and cloaks behind high walls
Men and women seeking inner calls
Checking it out one winter's day
Wondering if a message was left

AWARENESS
Aromas permeating reality
Purity of mind simmering below
Capping it off for future reference
I'll use it if my batteries ever run low

REALLY NEED
Watching passers by
Idling below your pool
Tailouts always provide
More than you really need

MADE IT BACK

Crackity crackity crak-ak
Big booms little booms-boom
Sounds of death and destruction
Some made it back by a gnat's ass

NO STONE

On another mission called out
Not quite as sketchy as our last
Me and my platoon in the vill
Leaving no stone or bag unturned

TOUR OR TWO

In this world of fickle people
Play's deceptions rule our days
You can find the no nonsense kind
Who've got a tour or two in their bag

DIG A LITTLE DEEPER

Going further within
Understanding what's without,
Our Creator's given His all
If you'd only remove your doubt.
Dig ye a little deeper
Uncovering hidden truths,
Lift up your brothers and sisters
Then shout it out from the roofs.
Go get yourselves together
Put petty bickering aside,
Rejoice in each others' visions
And seek the Holy tide.
Time ticks and tocks for thee
As futures come leaving fast,
So too sands in the hourglass
While days'n years go past.
You've got a lot to do
More than one really knows,
So go get out – get to it
Doing your part in
This heavenly cosmic show.
Don't be a quitter
Or one to play games,
Life's really a miracle
To waste it would be a shame.

THE CRITICS
Like stars on ice skating
No sinking line is required
You dance cavorting on the top
Until the critics gobble you up

MYTHIC PROPORTION
Old stories whispered about
Elders telling around fire's light
Youngsters with saucer-like eyes glowing
Listening to rainbows of mythic proportions

TROPHY
You're a real bruiser roger that
Long at the tape and heavy on my scale
With pretty wide shoulders and a big mouth
You pig, you toad, you trophy

HEAVY CREELS
Another day life's offer
Fishers roaming earth's wonder
With tips'n tricks'n heavy creels
But you shake your head just saying no

RED ROPES
Museum quality settings
With tickets none required
No red ropes to stay behind
With not a thing better to do

AGAINST A TREE
Spring waters rise and fall
Breathing life into all below
So I fill my cup to overflowing
While my pole leans against a tree

BIG SKY COUNTRY
Scouting out our next bigger trip
Fishing reports from local guides
Productive waters yes we've got 'em
Big sky country with miles of runs

STILLING MY MIND
Entering ancient realms
Secluded places like no other
Possibility of stilling my mind
Becomes much more than mere fantasy

THE AUDITION
Yellow disk prying into canyon's bed
Valleys begin to stretch then yawn
Our feathered friends go hmm hum
Warm ups for auditions to come

DO IT AGAIN

Streaming through the ether
Like a vegas showgirl,
Off to do your number
On glassy waters in time.
You've always come through
On a moment's notice,
Whatever your dress
Though I prefer marabou blue.
You must taste good
Or wag it just right,
Whatever your magic is
The boys sure put up a fight.
So I call you out
To do it again,
I know you won't complain
But we know where you've been.
You have done it all
Whole world's your stage,
Now go shake your booty and
Try not to break a leg.

LITTLE SIP
With plenty to drink
No need for a second round
Please pass the wings
As I could use a little sip

NIRVANA
Mountaintops off in the distance
Like dragon's spines without end
Every other range fishable water
I think nirvana's out there too

GETTING DIZZY
Steep trails and narrow paths
A maze of wonderment awaits
With so many to choose from
I'm getting dizzy on the natch

COSMIC SEA

My compass leads in seven directions
And our inner sense guides us well
Becoming one with this cosmic sea
Making hay in this precious life

THE DIVINE

A gray mist begins to rise
Mixing with bearers of life
You'll often see me out here
Rubbing elbows with the divine

FEAR NO EVIL

Gazing off into distant horizons
Dusk begins fading amid night's eye
Porch lights alight in valleys below
But I fear no evil with you at my side

PUT IT AWAY

The dogs of war unleashed again
Death or glory's in store for sure
How can we put it away for good
When there's so much money to be made

COME TO LIFE

Rain dancing off your poncho
Like a feeding frenzy rising
Taking cover in shaded woods
Watching it all come to life

CAKE'N ICE CREAM

Winds ride midday currents
Lake's beginning to unsettle
Roads to camp call out softly
Eating my cake'n ice cream too

YOU'LL KNOW WHEN

A country boy's calling
For red white and blue,
Been itch'in to get out of dodge
Travel round this world too.
You've put your time in
On ranch or farm and more,
Off to uncle's special office
Seeing what else's in store.
You looked at his list
Picking your MOS,
Signed on dotted lines…
So ready or not it's time.
Off to a port
Base, island or fort,
Then shit hits the fan
Better follow Lt.'s plan!
All the right drills,
And all the right scores,
Geared up ready for deployment
Time to knock down some doors.
Now that we're back,
(A little lighter of course)
Having given all that we had,
In case you were wondering:
You'll know when you've given enough
When you've given more than you can,
When you've given until it hurts.

ALREADY THERE
Dreams flying in mountain's rare air
Carrying you with circuitous routes
Signs, wonders, hints and signals
Waking up you're already there

EVERY CAST
The old adage holds and sways
What doesn't happen to kill you
Makes one appreciate each breath
Or in our case…every cast

DAZZLES MY MIND
A masterpiece with no paints
An artist who knows no equal
Our Creator splashing colors
Dazzling my mind with beauty

WHY WISH
Your road to perfection is long
You're standing on this very spot
The center of our universe is there
Why would you wish time went any faster

FIRST STEP
Mind's serpents play and frolic
Hiding'n seeking in gray matters
Subduing beasts within or without
Is the first step on heaven's road

THINGS TO COME
Walking for miles in forest's scene
On ways destined as pathless paths
My cup spilleth over having been
A precursor of things to come

FULLY LIVED
Fading light from sun's fingers glow
Casting his shadows on all below
While I sit here contemplating
Another day fully lived

AT MY LEISURE
Returning home life nearly forgot
Time distorted from action then
A slower march holds no grudge
Smelling manna at my leisure

MY EYES
Moon's burning cold and bright
Lighting ways to the left and right
With mists settling on troubled waters
Shading visions of darkness from my eyes

END OF DAYS

For thousands of years
You've enthralled us all,
Swimming and thriving
Answering our call.
Scientists tend to agree
Us two-legged types
Are relative newcomers,
To your ancient stage.
Cavemen built wooden traps
Flinging flint-tipped spears,
But us modern marvels
Have turned survival
Into high art.
Some say it's a worthless sport
Chasing elusive rainbows
Like in a watery dream,
Often coming home empty handed.
Little do these masses know
Of things we thus speak,
Punching in 9 − 5 :
Five days for fifty weeks.
No − O ye of little faith
You could not understand
Our serious ways,
God gave us two types of rainbows;
One as a promise and one as a gift
For everyone's delight
Until the end of days.

WONDERING
Sitting here pondering combat missions
On desolate slopes in my mind's eye
I'm wondering how many more years
We need to pull our heads out

NEW SPORT
Sun's last rays fall and linger
Doing a dance on mountain's peak
Starting to master this new sport
Hunting riverdogs instead of humans

TIGHTEN THE REIGNS
Rising at first light to begin another day
Journey's lifetime all work and some play
Minds try tugging like prancing monkeys
Tighten your reigns slowing them down

RIVER'S SONG
Emerald dimensions further than thought
Sights for sore eyes if ever needed be
Green trees free seas of tranquility
Where river's songs sing to souls

FILL MY NEEDS
Deeper reaches in realms unknown
Wilderness dreams call us out
Old friends welcome you back
Willing to fill your needs

TIME TO RELAX
You sing no songs nor tell no tales
Weaver of dreams and spinner of spells
Actually quite rare a diamond in the rough
Always tight-lipped but there's a time to relax

TEST YOUR METTLE
New rivers beckon and call
Realms hiding vast potential
Packing everything but the sink
Time to test your mettle once more

BAD INTENTIONS
You're a real sharp dresser
Really bright and look'in good
Would anybody have even considered
You'd slam flies with bad intentions

WORLD CLASS
Having been around globe's blocks
Now that we've finally made it home
Seems like everything's so different
World class with the pain to prove it

SAVE OUR WORLD

Swimming through worlds
Of shadowed rock,
We seek to and fro
For that perfect spot.
Our life's a dream
In suspended animation,
From coast to coast
In many a nation.
Chilling in pools of
Waters not so clear,
Waiting for a snack
While you sip your beer.
We dance the dynamic duel
As you and your kind,
Are seeking and searching
Hoping to find?
So now that we know
You're killing us all
With wreckless abandon for sure,
Won't you all please wise up
(Before it's too late)
And save our world,
We would do it
If we could.

MEET AGAIN
In distant fields
Of heavenly green
We'll meet again
Before too long

CUTTHROAT SAFARIS
Gearing up for unknown zones
Destinations across our globe
You were pretty good over there
Now it's cutthroat safaris or bust

CLOSED MIND
Into wilderness of earthly desires
Where you press on in unearthly fires
Thrills of otherworldly existence exceeds
All those choosing to possess a closed mind

MY WILL
Loud silence near dark wood's scream
Entering primordial awareness's dream
Where between atomic structures unseen
Manipulating reality conforms to my will

BAG OF TRICKS
Gazing from places of casual abundance
Objects on mirrors appear larger than life
Where a sense of powerlessness tends to prove
We need to dip down deeper in our bag of tricks

ABOVE AND BELOW
Hills growing from city's flats
On our way distant mountain tops
Slowing down getting into a groove
Becoming one with all above and below

LEG AND A DRUM

I could hear snowflakes falling
The silent sounds of old man winter
If only we hadn't been so close that day
Remote controlled death minus a leg and a drum

HEAVY HAND

Having been called to perform
Acts unmentionable in the village
How lucky those of us making it back
With our heavy hand of mercy and justice

THE OTHERSIDE

In the still of the night death comes calling
Who knows for sure if he will summon thee
Fertile lands on the otherside filling
Countless souls who long to be free

ONLY A TEST

Entering realms
Heavenly and divine,
Searching for phantoms
Both speckled and sublime.
This path we thus follow
Is hard to comprehend,
New conundrums await
Around every corner,
And nearly every bend.
Becoming aware of
Stations hard to grasp,
Unseen angels watch
Your every move,
Trying to guide
Our every step.
However hard
This road may seem,
It's really only a test,
So dig a little deeper
As they only accept the best.
Just in case you think
You've got what it takes,
Lifting up those nearest
Use both feet on the gas
And avoid your brakes.

MORE LIKE US

A wind's whistle in conifer forests
Sounds like the angels are saying
It's all right you had to do it
Now you are more like us

PRESENCE KNOWN

Past meadows over the rise
Sacred realms await all comers
Power spots of harmonic convergence
A place they make their presence known

IT MIGHT HELP

Along your local rivers fine days bloom
A new season arrives waiting for you
Go ahead and go get yourself in it
It might help you smell the dope

POLISH YOUR MIRROR
Worth more than tons of gold
Trips to mountains surely hold
Much more than meets mortal eyes
Polish your mirror wiping any dust

JUST DREAMING
Casting shadows moon's pale light
Glows and softens a harsh world
Perpetual music of rivers flow
Am I awake or just dreaming

WELCOME THEM
There's no best time to share your inner world
Thoughts and memories rarely if ever fade
Accept them like an innocent bystander
And welcome them like an old friend

ANY PLATE SERVED
With or without you heroes always go
Never needing to follow herd's lead
They step up to any plate served
Pretty much like you always do

PERCEIVED CHANGE
Bold winds come when least expected
Sometimes cold chills do follow
Adrift in creation's vastness
Welcome all perceived change

ONE THRU TEN
Full moons pulling white-capped froth
Gravitational persuasion disturbs rest
Getting an early start to beat the pack
Stilling my mind counting one through ten

PAY ANY PRICE

You're an acrobatic specialist
Rocking routines daily,
Working for less than peanuts
On stages far or near,
Though it'll cost us a pretty penny
If we want to come and see the show.
Fred and Ginger certainly
Got noth'in on you,
As your repertoire
Is virtually endless,
Most critics generally agree…
You're worth admission's price.
You always get top ratings,
What with your gobs of
Strength, style and heart,
Putting all others to shame.
Flying through the air
Tail-dancers on surface play,
Never need'in no stink'in nets
Cause your chops are down pat.
I'll pay any price
To watch you perform
And my lad won't complain
If there's no popcorn to be had.

FAST ENOUGH
In cities of life we ply our trades
For thousands of years and still today
You'd think an evolving race would get it
Evidently natural causes are not fast enough

MAGICAL KEY
New years come when old friends gather
Time sure seems to fly without any wings
Controlling perception is the magical key
That will unlock all your pain and suffering

GRAVEL BARS
Rendezvous points in city lights
Searching for that peace of mind
Me and my bros prefer gravel bars
As sports bars carry no fresh fish

FLASHES OF RED
In subtle rivers my dreams hold
Living visions with purple and gold
Where flashes of red are bandied about
Telling me to always seek the reel thing

CURRENT SEAMS
Between the fast and the slow
Many smorgasbord delights await
Casting what might be an appetizer
Current seams where any bills are paid

LOG JAMS
Sterile rivers without debris
A walk in the park sans the park
We all prefer nice vistas and shade
So try no to clear all our log jams

AT NIGHT

Pale moon fishers stalking
The biggest browns after dark
Why you ask not in the sunshine
Some of my best work's come at night

RHYTHM OF LIFE

As ice and frost begin to wane
Promises of spring call you again
Listen to your supersubconscious then
Your green light into rhythms of life

SHAKE IT OFF

Ten thousand directions from where I stand
Invisible forces are pulling me apart
This heavy load can weigh one down
So shake it off like a wet dog

SECRETS OF OLD

Riddles or rhymes,
Secret pools
With hidden finds,
Right after left
We toil along,
Fellow beings
Seeking happiness.
Simple pleasures
In mountains abound,
Keep lights bright
When I'm not around.
I'll be out in
God's vast abode,
Trying to unravel
The secrets of old.
I'm many years into
Trials so severe,
Waiting and watching
For His spirit to revere.
You might not notice
This sincerity in my aim,
Black robes'n purple cloaks
Say more than silence requires,
So be on the lookout for
One most humble and plain.

THE ONLOOKERS

On gilded walls in soldier's halls
Red carpets cover ivory towers
Where memories eagerly await
The onlookers standing at attention

ON THE NATCH

In fields of royal valor
Death was only a breath away
Where men were men on the natch
Beats borrowed from future recompense

MIGHTY ROAR

One journey completed another begins
Lack of inherent existence allows for all
With illusions of permanence permanently gone
I'm cutting through delusions with a mighty roar

LONG HAUL

Entering into earthly existence
A task not for any meek of heart
Pace yourselves for the long haul
It's best to err on caution's side

USE IT WISELY

Another season's on its way
Another season's come and gone
This gift that's been freely given
Pay attention always using it wisely

FATE OF NATIONS

Little ones resting and dreaming at ease
A country's soldiers don their stations
Hopefully our children wise ones be
Who'll change the fate of the nations

STOOD IN AWE

In desert scented dreams I've drifted
In wetter jungle canopies have fought
With action so fierce standing in awe
Wishing life were as intense as death

HOW MUCH LONGER

Flames have been snuffed out
Their wicks were cut too short
The price paid could build nations
How much longer will it take to learn

THOUGHTFORMS

With unlimited expanse at my disposal
I remove all doubts and weak links
Thoughtforms who know no bounds
Choosing good tossing the bad

THE WINNING TEAM

Vaporous mists arise
On bodies crystal clear,
Reflecting realms afar
However close or near.
This life we thus lead
Never for ones afraid to part,
It's been written about for ages
Before the beginning had it's start.
So tread your path carefully
Between righteousness and dark,
Ominous warnings surround
Not your average song from a lark.
We teach by example
Cause He showed us His way,
Of numerous other paths
This is the shortest one I know.
So if you dare
To travel along,
Grab your pole
Singing our song;
Sons of Zadok
Fishers of trout and men,
It's where you're going
Not where you've been,
So come on over then
And join the winning team.

LITTLE DRAGON
Caverns near poolside eddys
In undercuts wherever they be
There you sit patiently waiting
Like a little dragon in your lair

ANCIENT WATERS
You're a worthy opponent obviously
One who always answers our call
So we meet on ancient waters
To see who takes the cake

THE HATCH
In anticipation of phenomena
Coming alive and thriving
Parked patiently waiting
For the hatch to arrive

TAKING NOTES
You've got the action just right
Working one more perfect retrieve
Three or four cranks with a twitch
Wondering if anyone is taking notes

SHARPSHOOTER
Having waited a short lifetime
Our country's call came knocking
Just three months out of high school
Sharpshooters looking for fresh targets

HOW COME
How many more bags need filled
How much more blood be spilled
How many more stripes go under
How come you just don't get it

GIVING BACK

Bust'in caps in combat zones
Load'in birds in cargo holds
Blazing L.Z.s in fires then
Giving back what's been given

LIFT ME UP

If we seem out of order
Kind'a dizzy things undone
Offering a hand lifting us up
I wasn't born to do what we did

NEXT LEVEL

Soldiers get the nod
To do what must be done
If only we'd pull together
We might get to the next level

OF COURSE

You're my favorite stick
Always ready and willing
To crack your whip,
From bank to bank
Where water of life is found.
You're a straight shooter
With hardly a curve,
Unless of course
You are loaded up
Doing a loop,
Or on the set
With a riverdog
Dancing at your tip.
You always come through
Even in deep
Remote destinations,
Never saying no
Rain or shine.
There are many more
Just like you,
But you are mine
And we have made
A pretty fine couple,
That is of course
When my wife
Was not around.

RIVERDOGS
Thin film surface tension floating
Like I'm in suspended animation
Trying not to twitch a muscle
Too many riverdogs prowl'in

BOULDER STREWN STREAM
Smooth roads sailing along
Like I'm in a blue coup deville
It was very explosive over there
Now I prefer boulder strewn streams

RAINBOWS UNDER WATER
Into my bag of tricks
Up and down down and up
You think this guy's crazy
Jigging for rainbows under water

WORTH MORE
Crimson skies crying
Another day punches out
Jade green soothes my soul
Worth more than fields of oil

ANOTHER WORLD
Stripers are nice and walleyes too
But I prefer one with a bit more class
In cool mountain settings are found
Redsides that take me to another world

NEW LIFE
Celestial presence fades into dawn
While I carefully kindle new life
The one we left was real spooky
Live like there's no tomorrow

FLUFFY BEARDS
After a long day on slippery slopes
Twenty miles into valleys never mapped
Moon plays hide and seek with fluffy beards
Better get some shut eye so I can beat the birds

HEAVY BURDEN
Flowers fallen in fields of fire
Heavy tolls ringing without cease
This country carries a heavy burden
Some of it is buried six feet under

NEVER FORGOTTEN
I tap the tip on watery rocks
Our last mission comes to mind
We spoke about this spot over there
Though gone you'll never be forgotten

UNIVERSAL SOLDIER

You've been in the shit
Time after time back then,
Life hung by a thread
You and your buddies
Between life's death:
Between hope's sin.
You've seen more
Than your fair share,
More than human eyes
In thin mortal skin
Have any right to bear.
You've done the unforgiven
Cause it had to be done,
Amid earth's fine veil,
In between heaven and hell.
It's a crime in most realms
But what can one man do,
Petty tyrants high'n drunk
When soldiers get a nod
To bring our balance back.
Call it what you will
Always keep the faith,
You're a universal soldier
Wherever you may roam…
And as we all know
A tired man never cares.

HOT L.Z.
Pastel patterns fade into life
Dew glistens on mossied floor
Breeze lifts breakfast's fire
Like rotors in a hot L.Z.

TIME TO TIME
On manicured lawns marble shimmers
Resting places settings in stone
We come here from time to time
Making sure it wasn't a bad dream

ONCE AGAIN
Approaching another village some locals gathered
How many friendlies this time one never knew
Setting a perimeter we shake'm all down
Wishing once again we'd all get along

DONE RIGHT
Celebrating life without a few friends
Those in the know with mist in their eyes
It's too bad it's come down to this though
Who do you call when you need it done right

HIGHLY OVERRATED
Soldiers of fortune for nations do stand
Ready and willing to answer any calling
Once you've been in the duff knee deep
You realize it's highly overrated

SHINY OBJECTS
22:00 and rucks are loaded
Mags topped all tags are taped
No shiny object to attract light
Rather not catch charlie's attention

NO LIMIT

Childhood memories tipping scales
Some to the left, some to our right
Adding them to other new experiences
Your heavenly credit card has no limit

WATCH AND WAIT

Human folly with idle chatter
Sitting back we watch and wait
In fields below unearthly realms
Hoping they'll get to the next level

NO MORE

Gear's checked in and birds put away
On our way back to the states again
Another mission's finally undone
Hoping we'll be called no more

BEFORE IT'S GONE

Rippling currents
And babbling brooks,
Kings'n queens with
Pawns and rooks,
A sport for royals'n commoners
No matter how you slice it.
Mountain meadows meandering
Playing like there's not to lose,
Calculating with precision
Each and every move.
This game of life we live
Between subliminal or sublime,
Me and my young ones cavorting
Enjoying then stilling time.
We come here often
To build the bond some more,
Our Creator's treasure chest
(Filled with all you'll want)
More than words will ever afford.
So put it on your list
Tippy-top if life you wish
Were a little more fulfilling,
I can assure all my friends
This is one tasty dish that
Must be tried before it's gone.

MYRIAD OPPORTUNITIES
New buds shooting towards heaven's hand
Springtime gives myriad opportunities
Pretty much like his other cousins
Summer and autumn and winter

EXPLODE WITH LAUGHTER
Cities of life aren't free from pain
Good days and bad come'n go like rain
When sitting down to analyze situations
I explode with laughter and pass it along

THE ILLUSION
Palace halls stand marble pillars
Kings and queens with guillotines
Plenty of pain for their peasants
Trying to keep the illusion alive

TEACH THE CHILDREN WELL

Ten thousand miles waiting to be fished
Whole upper northwest like heaven on earth
Now that we've done more than our fair share
Time to settle down and teach the children well

MIRACULOUS EVENTS

In far away lands of mist and rain
Invisible forces where dragons once laid
With tales that speak of miraculous events
The place you can go to keep your spirit alive

MIDDLE WAY

Walking illusions some pleasure mostly pain
Rich and famous appearing to have it made
Seeking the middle way for peace of mind
When others stumble I lend them a hand

THIS FAR

Now that I've begun understanding life's loves
Childhood ambitions where green grass grows
I've made a step back taking a harder look
Realizing miracles of making it this far

PRICE WE PAID

Going north by northwest by far away lands
Resting with shadows amid mystic rivers
The price we paid to enjoy God's gifts
Was quite a bit higher than listed

VERDANT DIMENSIONS

In verdant dimensions I travel through
My raiment was soaked by coastal fog
Faint voices spoke off in the distance
On my way back home to realms unknown

ANTICIPATION

The night before an early rise
Often hard drifting to dreams,
Anticipation of morning's thrill
Sometimes more than one person can bear.
(Tossing & turning) – (plotting and planning)
Each bend in mountain's jewel
With whole forests as your witness,
Knowing full well what challenges await.
Finally you glimpse precognitions
Adventures yet to come,
If only reality were as bright as
Vivid rivers you fished in the night,
What a wonderful world this would be.
Zero-dawn thirty:
When moments arrive,
Your week's work
Is finally paying off.
You've done it before
Perhaps one thousand times,
You could do it blindfolded
But it would never be
Quite as much fun.

RIVER OF LIFE
Numbing chills crept up upon us
Ancient runs were about to arrive
Gathering weapons for tasks at hand
My buddies and I in this river of life

CLOUDS IN THE SKY
Tired memories knocking on interior doors
Are they trying to get out or go back in
Whatever their invisible motives might be
I watch them pass like clouds in the sky

ON THE LINE
Application after application till I'm blue in the face
Walking and knocking down doors all over this place
How many more no's is one expected to endure
If only they knew the lengths I would go

OUR MIND

Bootcamp instills subtleties beyond compare
Young persons transformed all new and rare
Eternity can't be kept hidden for long
Like your mind which encompasses it all

INNUENDOES AND IMPRESSIONS

Ethereal hands from on high reach
And voices unseen louder than drums
Subtle innuendoes and impressions do come
You need a still mind to decipher their codes

SO SWEET

Travelling away from home again
To greener pastures with a friend
Off to spots of unthinkable delights
Who would have thunk life was so sweet

NEVER CHANGE

Keeping citizens blind and folded
Hustling and bustling scurrying along
Reality being just another illusional song
Maybe it's why some things never seem to change

PLACE WE GO

Freshly smoked trout's hard to forget
Homemade brews with foam'n heady scents
Where mother nature always treats us well
This place we go not as often as we should

MY VOICE

Feathered ones chatter in forest's dreams
Busily going about their daily lives
Like me singing while I whittle
Hoping angels will recognize my voice

OUR OWN DEMISE

Cooped up in cages
And grayed cityscapes,
Hardly a tree in sight
Nor streams or rivers or lakes.
Huddling masses existing
In troubled dirty streets,
Rumbling'n mumbling
While shuffling their feet.
What a life to live to –
What a life to die to –
You might change your fate
If you wise up and try too.
See the future is unwritten
A story that's not been told,
You can make a difference
(If you choose to)
Like manna in fields of gold.
It's up to you
It's you make the call,
For we can stand up forever
Pulling together as a team,
Or perish in our own ignorance
(Surely not very wise)
One more manmade fall
Another wasted chance
Of our own demise.

ONE STEP
Daydream reverie of wishful things
Nighttime visions in the memory bank
Awaking I take one step after another
Letting my actions speak for themselves

AS IT APPEARS
Shrugging my shoulders when asked the question
Who really knows hidden meanings of things
But I'm taking solace understanding that
Everything isn't as it appears to be

IN PLAIN SIGHT
Grabbing my stick heading for mountains deep
Walking meditations while I figure it out
Anticipating answers often found there
Hiding in plain sight for all to see

NEVER LEFT

Not long gone but never forgotten
Molecules fade into new adventures
How sad it appears you've departed
If only we realized you never left

WASTE NO TIME

Seasons dance in the fabric of space
Another one's here only for a minute
How many more do you have to witness
Better get up early and waste no time

ULTIMATE GOALS

On yon edge of thundering mountain lakes
Many thoughts fade into relative nothingness
Loosening their grasp on conventional reality
Where ultimate goals become a little more vivid

PERFECT IMPOSTER

Floating on winds new cities arriving
Billions of creatures living webs of life
Sitting back contemplating conundrums
Into your tin house for a perfect imposter

THE TRAIL

Heading upriver seeking your source
Living waters bigger and better things
Learning to decipher unanswerable answers
I've found the trail where my sojourn begins

NEW KIDS

Flying objects in night skies fly
From where they come a mystery be
How many eons must they have been
We being the new kids on the block

THE HUNTER HUNTING

Stroke after stroke and
Breath after breath,
Tranquil waters waving
Mirroring heaven's eye.
Heave after ho and
Ho after heave,
Warming my muscles
In blizzard's conditions.
Bald eagle came calling
Scouting his next meal,
Mt. Shasta stood guard
Of reality so surreal,
Two buddies and I
Gliding through nirvana
Without ever speaking a word.
Some say motors are nice
But they break magic's spell,
Both above and below:
Too much noise to hear
The hunter hunting.

NO ONE KNOWS
Clouds of antimatter swirl in my mind
Thirty-three outings to hell and back
This purple path keeps calling me out
How long it'll take no one knows

STANDING TALL
Having been to the black-etched stone
A piece in time for eternity's eyes
The soldiers' names who reside there
Standing tall so no one forgets

BETWEEN THE LINES
Temples with two legs go then falter
Idle minds gathering grow much moss
Seeking the unknown via the known
Trying to read between the lines

CHUG SOME JOE
On the tour bus another village
Dragon's breath permeates reality
Two hours until our patrol departs
Better chug some joe and shake it off

IF ONE BLINKED
Unnoticed actions of heroes here and there
Each mission survived more miracles witnessed
Angels on constant and perpetual watch up above
But if one ever blinked bad things usually happened

PERFECT IMITATION
Standing in shade near woodland's edge
Little bits of cover by water's ledge
Where I tie on the perfect imitation
Trying to imitate the fisher of men

NEVER LEAVE

Into oblivion sun's bright chariot rides
Who knows when or if he'll ever return
Like us here for a minute or three
Only to realize we never leave

SWING OF THINGS

Big mountains there tall ones watch
Rushing rivers fingers flowing freely
Where one can go to enliven foggy heads
And ease back on into the swing of the things

RIVERS OF CHANGE

Riding waves, hopes and dreams
Seas of life in rivers of change
Polishing my board I hit the beach
Trying not to blow any onlookers' minds

NEVER FADE

One more time
On waters so divine,
Searching for phantoms
Others fail to find.
Knowing you're out there
In cool pools abound,
I'm on a mission
With gps in hand.
From the north to the south
And all over this planet,
Have no fears you
Slippery little fellow,
For when we meet
It won't be your last,
I'm not so vain as to
Take you from your home.
No – this I will not do!
I'll hold you gently
Plucking your fateful snack,
Though I might be quick
To take a shot or two
So the memory of our dance
Will never fade.

COSMIC SHOW
Gentle currents in valleys go
Blue skies shining for all below
Where new life begins and does grow
I shine like a gem in this cosmic show

I WONDER
Berries dot paths to my favorite spot
It's good to get away whenever I can
Keys and clues'n treasures galore
I wonder if it gets any better

CITY LIFE
Entering into oceans of bliss
One more time in natural worlds
City life can be okay for a week
If I disappear you know where I'm at

DAILY HABIT

When winter's grip loses her hold
Opening day's right around the bend
Visiting my bench on a regular basis
Seems to have become another daily habit

SWEET MUSIC

Springtime walking from south to north
Carrying handfuls of colors looking busy
Birds and bees seem to follow their leads
After they've arrived sweet music follows

SLOW CURRENT

Fast water's fine
In freestone's tight line
Chalk streams too
But I prefer a slow current

PERPETUAL BLISS
When kindred spirits finally meet
Where life's sweeter than tupelo honey
One can finally begin to enter into
States of perpetual bliss

EVERY TIME
Scattered across this earthly abode
Enigmas and puzzles with green so bold
Seeking and searching hidden ways of old
Every time I look down there it is

PLAIN TO SEE
Fall colors begin to wane
Mother nature does it again
I look forward to winter's kiss
Plain to see if you open your mind

MOUNTAIN STORE

Dodging shrapnel and bullets
With occasional i.e.d.'s,
Working through green zones
Not your average walk in the breeze.
We're fighting for freedom
Keeping tyrants at bay,
Hoping to make it home soon
So me and my boy can play.
I'll take him to his river
Near lakes on mountain's store,
Right around the corner from
Grandpa's favorite shore.
It's a nice place to go,
It's a nice place to fish,
If you be still'n quiet there
Someone just might catch their wish.
The sights'n sounds as I remember
Days gone by well spent,
My dad's dad discovered it
And it's where we'll have gone and went.
My boy's growing up fast,
My boy's grow'in up strong,
My wife sure wants a daughter though
Think I'll help her along.
So if you see us one fine day
In forested hills'n dales,
Know that our family paid your price
A real tight unit that's got the goods.

BLACKBIRD
Caw caw caw ravens prattling on
Intelligent forms in forests dwell
Wondering if their relatives one did
Ride the shoulders of an ancient uncle

RAINCHECK
Our weaver wove a tapestry of webs
Signs and signals for all to ponder
Who knows when and how this all began
I'm glad not to have gotten a raincheck

FAVORITE TOME
Sitting amidst amorphous chaos
Labyrinths and portals prophesy
Clouds drifting translucent skies
Reading the signs in my favorite tome

EVEN IF
Reading weather's invisible report
Fisherman's almanac'n barometer's bet
Anticipating a day in little heaven
And go even if the signs say no

GONNA TRIP
Early day dawns floating between
Life or death and silly day dreams
Lacing up my boots with a double knot
Not gonna trip on any bumps in the road

SAME CLAN
Meeting fellow fishers ten miles in
Rare events encountered now and then
Stopping we chat about life's journeys
Silently knowing we're from the same clan

DREAMS AND DESIRES

Rolling out blowing on moon's embers
Kids in pup-tents big dreams and desires
Boiling cold water getting their cups filled
Sprinkling cocoa and prayers for things to come

HIGH ON LIFE

Constellations gliding above thin clouds
A chorus singing silent night aloud
Presence of cosmic forces abound
Where I go to get high on life

IN THE KNOW

In crazy times mostly for show
Many people primp and prime and go
Shallow pools with tons of hot air blow
While those of us who know uphold our world

WIZARD OF CAUSE

Cold, clouds,
Wind then rain,
Please watch my back
While I do magic things.
I'm off to see a wizard
The wonderful wizard of cause,
So old no one remembers His name
Nor figure out His immutable laws.
See, there are things unknown
And things meant to wonder,
But age old questions
Which came first:
A fish or an egg,
Takes too much time to ponder.
Just pass my pole
Then a little bit of bait,
I'm head'in for our hole
Cause we've got a hot date.
See, time's real precious
And there's never enough of it,
It's off to chase some rainbows
With the wonderful wizard of cause.

FUTURE'S SO BRIGHT
Hoping to witness a big event
Next day dawns from one that went
Putting on shades dulling the dazzle
Future's so bright better grab my backup

WHAT IT TAKES
Seekers of trout
And fishers of men
Dark forces tempt you
Cause you got what it takes

AS I REMEMBER
Many moons the pain's still there
In far away places playing G.I. Joe
Remembering it was quite a bit funner
When I was four or five and no one died

WHEEL OF LIFE
Springtime's waters rise
Flowers beginning to bloom
Each one getting another go
On the wheel of life we ride

FOOD FOR THOUGHT
No need to rehash tired memories
What's been done still stirs the soup
Some of our bowls are better than others
All in all providing more food for thought

WISHING WELL
Long or short straws no one knows
Life begins in humble bags of bones
The primordial essence in which we dwell
Gets to dance and play in His wishing well

A CUT ABOVE
Standing tall while others bend and buckle
Forged in fires bare bones and knuckles
Passing any test they threw at us
Those of us there a cut above

WONDERFUL OPPORTUNITY
Winter's cloth gray and white
Off seasons when life slows down
Wonderful opportunity to hop on over
And loiter with your friends for a while

ANOTHER MASTERPIECE
Waking up at dawn to squeeze a few more drops
Life's so sweet a palette that never stops
With a menu beyond mortal comprehension
Waiting to create another masterpiece

LITTLE DECEIVER

You're my other favorite
All snuggled up
In your tin house,
Waiting for us
To ring your bell.
You kick it nicely
With your brothers
And sisters all
Dressed up and
Ready to ride.
You never ask questions
Or complain about conditions,
You're an eager participant
Just waiting to salute.
So I ring the bell
Opening your door,
Where you faithfully leap
Into my frozen fingers,
Always ready to deceive
You little deceiver.

ROAD OF LIFE

Traveling roads of life we go
Smelling flowers as they grow
Sun rides watching us glow
I dance even in the rain

BIG PICTURE

Dancing winds leading partners
Entire forest rocks and grooves
Sitting here patiently observing
Beginning to grasp the big picture

FAMILY BOND

BBQ smoke wafting all around
Kids cavorting constant motion
Visiting this best place on earth
Our family bond gets a little stronger

EVERY TRICK
You run and play in the deep and the shallow
Hiding behind glacial boulders and rocks
Where I use every trick in my playbook
Inventing new ones just to keep up

YOU NEVER KNOW
With a mystery report bordering on a who did it
Partly cloudy mostly sunny light to raw gusts
Lose your radio always packing for extremes
Like life you never know what you'll get

I AM
Standing in alpine shadows
Vast vistas welcome your eyes
Contemplating this great expanse
Knowing I am at the center of it all

GREEN ZONE
From favorite campsites where woods run deep
Rear areas rested preparing for things to come
This green zone is fragrant from my new position
No hint of fuel or blood bringing back old memories

COVERED IN DEW
As the bringer of life wakes us all
Unzipping our tent covered in dew
A soft breeze greets morn's dawn
Mouths water preparing the fire

FEED YOUR SOUL
Thick shade hovers on canyon's wall
Deep pockets hold more than gold
Places to go and feed your soul
Hunting for better things now

SPREAD YOUR WINGS

Another long week
Working for my bread
Heading for some hills
Recharging these batteries
Clearing my foggy head.
The times we are live'in
Certainly quite thrilling,
If only we'd start spreading
Peace, love and compassion,
Maybe we'd stop all the killing?
Doing my best I do my part
Not adding needless chaos,
9-5, five days a week
Then for three months...
Little league on our weekends.
There's a slight chance
You know what I mean,
With a load that's quite heavy
Being where you've been,
And seeing what you've seen.
So do something nice
For yourself for a change,
Get out with mother nature
Wet your line and
Spread your wings.

SOME SNACKS

Light workouts before first glimpse
Only eight hours on to pay our bills
When I get home it's cold brew thirty
Heading for my bench to tie some snacks

THE PAYOFF

Learning to love these precious gifts
Another day brings countless rewards
Even while I toil to make it happen
The payoff is hard to comprehend

ALL ONE

Flowered meadows'n critters on the peek
Invisible mover moves without moving
Like innate wisdom guiding us all
All one in this heavenly play

A FEW BROS

Out pops topo planning our next trip
Idle time building stronger bonds
Where the family and I often go
And a few brothers tag along

FUTURE GREATNESS

Getting closer snow covered peaks
Children stir, come alive and thrive
With imaginations that know no bounds
A place where we build future greatness

PASSED DOWN

Grassy meadows rocky mountains high
Off to the spot that gramps showed me
Pleasures of unimaginable delights await
A gift passed down for generations to come

PLATOON MEMBER
Getting ready for our yearly outing
Platoon members from fields of fire
Looking back we count the blessings
Making sure it doesn't happen again

PATIENT OBSERVER
Sowing gardens in forest's pine
Small temples in harm's way goes
Slowing down long enough who knows
What wonders await patient observers

COMFORTING GLOW
Fading light casts long shadows
Horizons fade into a blue-black
The eyes of a billion universes
Bat then wink a comforting glow

WATERS

They say trout waters
Falling from heaven's bed,
Are the purest about
This earthly abode.
And snows melting
From peaks so proud,
Are the next best
Below heavenly cloud.
Calm waters dwelling
In caverns dark'n deep,
Found springing forth
From Gaia's earthly keep,
Certainly takes no back seat.
Wherever it comes from
Really matters not,
Just keep it clean and
Give me more of it.

INNER LIGHT

Morning mists on rivers of being
With gray skies lining heaven above
The muted presence of life's dance dulls
But my inner light shines like a thousand suns

IMMORTALITY

People of the earth traveling
On a blue marble do they ride
Between your birth and death
Immortality's key is found

IDLE CHATTER

Never understanding secret societies
Old geezers in gilded halls plotting
Global domination under wisdom's guise
We can see it's definitely idle chatter

ALL CONNECTED
Battles and conflicts ten thousand miles away
Butterflys beginning their journeys flapping
Causing turbulent weather on the other side
More proof that it's all connected

LET IT GO
Mission's done and a few friends are gone
Left with vivid memories of both still fill
Waking daydreams plus unpleasant nightdreams
Will somebody please teach me how to let it go

COUNTING BLESSINGS
Looking high into starlight at night
An autumn chill permeates this sphere
Staring skyward in wonderment of it all
Counting blessings is my new full-time job

BEDTIME STORY

Another long day draws to a close
While earth and stars reach to greet
The silver moon dances in her element
And little ones await their bedtime story

SWEET TUNE

Morning fogs begin to lift
Birds hum another sweet tune
Singing and chirping as they work
Many moons never seeing a happier lot

ME AND HIM

Deep into backcountry
Sitting high atop a peak
Pondering the imponderable
Me and Him chatting till dawn

SLIPPERY LITTLE FRIENDS

I've recalled
When I was young,
Longing for answers
Greater than my self.
A mystery unseen
Beyond mortal grasp,
With hopes'n dreams
So off I went to roam.
This dirty world
Big city lights
Wasn't for me,
Then I went
And made my own.
Over many a sea
For greater goods,
They said it was
The right thing to do.
Now that we're back
I hunt riverdogs
In forest glens,
As the enemy without
Is not greater than
Our enemy within.
Because of that
I thank you all
For helping me out
My slippery little friends.

2 LB. TEST

Mile after mile and valley after valley
The serious trekker makes their mark
With rucks loaded for bear and
A hot-rod with 2 lb. test

CLICK AWAY

Back in some boonies our yearly trip
Me and my boys like old times again
Where action was only a click away
This time everyone makes it home

DOGGIE BAGS

When opening day comes alive
Wet ones realize their jig is up
All of a sudden the buffet arrives
With enough doggie bags to go around

COLD BREW

Salad and chicken wings for supper
With a cold brew to wash it all down
It's off to bed early because tomorrow
I'll be serving wings sans meat and bones

LITTLE CHIPMUNKS

Chattering waves lick polished rock
Lap after lap like primordial hearts
Little chipmunks barking their orders
And blue jays check all guests' tickets

BOYS FROM NAM

Long lost loved ones congregating at gates
Offering up small tokens of appreciation
Luckily they show no signs of contempt
Like our boys from nam had to endure

UP ABOVE
Fir-needle mattress under a sparkling sky
Melodies of delight murmuring nearby
While watching movements up above
I wonder what's really going on

NOTH'IN TO IT
Awoken for last watch before reveille
Like rising for early morning trips
Into turquoise falls river's call
I go like there's noth'in to it

COMMON SENSE
Public officials on high horses ride
Daily banter over red and the blue
Will common sense one day prevail
Maybe we'll save this planet yet

NORTH COUNTRY

Flashes, swirls'n thumps
But you're not on the feed,
Must've been out late
All I feel is a few bumps.
Winding up my loop then
Dropping in above your lane,
Split-bamboo working like magic
Rise forms rise again.
You're idling in the cut
Waiting for something to slurp,
I work some shade and cover
Picking up for another cast,
While my boy's on the bank
Enjoying moments that last.
We're in your north country
Up near heaven's sky,
Wind whispers in wooded wonders
Hunting fish with speckled skin
Priceless memory making,
No need to reason why.
So go get yourself in it.
Feeling what it's all about,
Cause once you taste this water
Then you'll know my friend…
You are alive!

WEEK AHEAD
Up near headwaters of my favorite creek
A thin place in hills I roam and seek
Where city life looks good from afar
Clearing my mind for the week ahead

POLAROID FILM
Sitting on mantles brothers in arms
Half-wide smiles with eyes that sweep
Back in the days when death came calling
And some made it back on thin Polaroid film

PLENTY TO DO
With a couple billion connections sitting atop your neck
A supercomputer that can and does rise to all occasions
Where clarity and insights just go with the territory
Constantly calculating conundrums I never get bored

EFFORTLESS EFFORT
Yesterday's troubles seem to consume
Going with the flow I left them behind
Just when you think it's a losing battle
Effortless effort overcomes all obstacles

US POETS
Between relative and ultimate reality abounds
With a constant influx of flotsam and jetsam
More ammo than all the bloody wars combined
Us poets fight to save this human race

PURE ENERGY
Trips into the past etched in bone
Gray mattered memories bright'n true
Remembering events with us chosen few
Realizing it's pure energy now and then

HOOT OF A FRIEND
Fire's life beginning to dim
Settling in for another world
Putting some hot ones in my bag
A friend hoots and wishes me well

BUCKLE DOWN
Once a short mortal lifetime
Begins to become more apparent
Moon and stars look a bit brighter
Best buckle down and make an impression

IMPERMANENCE
On a winter's night herbal tea simmers
One last cup before dream world wins
Long days dancing with impermanence
A cosmic show that's just started

SNEAKY LITTLE DEVIL

Sun rises over mountain's forest
As captains holding helm
Anticipate your next move,
Making richest men from the poorest.
It's another adventure in realms unknown
Sneaking'n stalking through carpets of rock,
Creeping and crawling with whispered talk.
This prey we thus seek
Is a sneaky little devil,
Breathing air under water
Hard to glimpse but always reel level.
We've put our time in
Through valleys'n canyons'n more,
Hunting a creature with no legs
Rainbows of colors never a bore.
It's really quite thrilling
Hinted in tales of yore,
One more time with gramps
As we closed shop early
Locking the back door.

SAME PAGE
Caught between darkness and light
Seven billion with no end in sight
Who know who's wrong or who's right
I'm praying we'll get on the same page

YODA-LIKE ACTION
Clear minds in a very dusty world
Clarity's contentment settles upon
The hustle and bustle and status quo
With Yoda-like action I make my stand

OLD AND NEW
Unveiling the clouds of unknowing
This inner wisdom I cultivate daily
With some help of masters old and new
Seeking immortality on my favorite path

WEAVE YOUR WEB

Life and death hold no claim on this spirit
From the moment you're born ends are near
No one knows how many moons you'll view
Weave your web for your immortal soul

NEW OPPORTUNITIES

Immersed within this fabric of space
Even the tiniest deserves awe and wonder
Every day many opportunities rise and fall
Without diversity there's no room for expansion

OTHER TOOLS

Trading in my bench for a desk
With more space for some other tools
I only need a corner for the vise anyway
More elbowroom to create these songs for you

LIGHT OF DAY

Across our nation a swell does grow
Same old same old's seen better days
A new crew of green-eyed earth lovers
Is starting to see bright light of day

TWO THOUSAND YEARS

Boisterous banter from roosters on hills
Each one clucking to be the cock of the walk
Where humbleness and righteousness are ill fated
It's only taken two thousand years to get this far

STEPPING STONES

No need to turn back half way on ascending journeys
Obstacles and adversities merely stepping stones
Each bump in our road hones insight and wisdom
You were born to toil so do it with grace

ONE MORE TIME

Running with my line
Faster than you can,
A little hand to hand
In afternoon's sun.
You stalk your prey to live
I stalk you for fun,
We really do a number
You, me and my son.
This joy you give us
A little hard to explain,
Maybe it's in the genetics
Somewhere deep in our brain?
So thanks for your service
Memories we'll surely share,
Now go get yourself back in it
And raise more than you can bear.
No matter the reason,
No matter the rhyme,
We'll be back next season
To do it one more time.

NATURAL ENERGY

Echoes of invisible winds speak and blow
For most people it only agitates and stirs
But those in the know surely relish its flow
Heightening your senses using natural energies

SELFLESS SELF

Unfocused attention in flurious action
Like wild horses that refuse their halter
Minds buck snorting from outside influence
Be ye mindful cultivating your selfless self

THOSE WHO KNOW

Smooth even strokes our quest begins
First steps into lifetimes with no end
Sometimes this goal is too hard to fathom
But those of us who know say left right left

SEE THE TRUTH
Silver inlaid visions line our night life
And ordinary ho hum colors every day dreams
Where one must work hard to see hidden truth
Turning chaff less wheat into nourishing manna

ALL THIS TIME
Silent sounds of night call the day
Adventurous outings with mother nature
As springtime comes but once a year finally
Little friends patiently waiting all this time

ON THE REEL
Sitting amongst giants near bejeweled ribbons
Already putting three hours in on the reel
Our stew's simmering over a bed of coals
Enlisting my pen I capture this moment

DUTY CALLS
After several tours the world still spins
Sun and moon work without a pot to piss in
Although it's hard appreciating past actions
What's a soldier supposed to do when duty calls

MORNING ROUTINE
Alarms at dawn sing my favorite songs
Slipping from one dream world to another
Morning routines before the day's awakened
Settling our minds effortless effort prevails

NEVER ASK
Into dimensions of ten million rivers and lakes
Countless streams and creeks calling from afar
If only my day job weren't so darn persistent
Out here I would never ask for any time off

SECRET WEAPON

O ye of feathered fare
You'd flap your wings
If you had any,
But you're all tied up
Jammed up jelly tight,
Flying through our air
With the greatest of ease.
You're in the bigtime now,
Off my vise and ready for battle.
You possess colors so bright
With your sword glistening
In caster of shadows' arms.
I picked you especially
For the task at hand
Requires a special soldier,
One willing to fly
And do some dirty work.
You're my secret weapon
So go on get at it
Plying your trade,
When my supper's finished
I'll tell you how you did.

COSMIC PUZZLE

On this ship of fools immortals in training
Spirits in a material world most don't know
With the beginning of creation so far back
A cosmic puzzle that may never be solved

ABIDE IN AWARENESS

Longing for spring to return once more
And wishing for it not to depart so fast
Those on point abide in awareness knowing
That permanence equals obstacles to growth

SITTING STILL

Having presence of mind to feel your potential
Daily missiles coming in from all seven directions
Sitting still deciphering questions out of thin air
Hoping to figure it out so you don't have to come back

EACH ATOM
With opened eyes versus closed minds
The every day world appears a dull gray
Once you learn to see beauty in each atom
You'll have more than 365 good days per year

ALL PHENOMENA
Once one becomes one with His way
Worry and anxiety are enemies no more
All phenomena get invited to the party
Any bringer of bad news no longer arrives

LIKE ME
After two tours with a broken marriage
A handful of odd jobs here and there
Stars'n planets fulfill their duty
Like me always gett'in 'er done

SAME CLOTH
In the ends the high'n the mighty
Share similar fates as us common men
How many more generations will it take
To see we're all cut from the same cloth

WHATEVER IT TAKES
Rain swelling rivers to overflowing
As soon as water clears it's all good
Now I'm planting invisible things growing
Doing whatever it takes to reap the harvest

IT'S OBVIOUS
Ancient lawns overrun with mementoes
Small tokens to never forget our fallen
After thousands of years of silly nonsense
Obviously we're evolving slower than we think

GIANTS OF THE FOREST

Standing on yonder's edge
Flowing manna here and there,
Sentinels of ancient's domains
Constantly on perpetual watch.
You filter the air we breath
Shading our eyes from bright light,
Always whistling while you work
Singing invisible songs.
You've witnessed countless events
Underneath your branches galore,
Feeding squirrels'n chipmunks
Giving birds all they need or more.
You hold precious banks together
Which no deposits are required,
These banks I thus refer to
Hold golden rainbows of heart's desire.
You're our giants of the forests
Keepers of life-giving ways,
For hundreds of years at a time
You watch and wait and play.

KING'S RANSOM
Tear-stained cheeks of those who greet
Big birds return bodies in darkened rooms
Vivid drapery donning their private palace
Is anybody tired of seeing this king's ransom

WIDE OPEN
Having been there and back we go where we want
Early morning showers bring aromatic flowers
With one and half legs and a sharp mind
Whole world's wide open and we're on it

STEADY PACE
Inspiration ebbs then flows like moths to flames
Fame and fortune is nice if your inner bank's full
Working the crowd for cheap applause the vain ones go
So me and my bros keep our heads down and a steady pace

QUANTUM ENTANGLEMENT
Sitting on a log in the great wide open
Yellow orb falling down feeds all around me
Realizing only illusional boundaries surround us
Little and big atoms quantum entanglement salutes

COUNTRY MILE
Me and my boy head into an unknown
Hungry tike's bouncing on mom's trail
Even though he's ten feet in front of me
I know his smile's wider than a country mile

HIDDEN DIMENSIONS
Evergreens cool forest's floor
Shading us from prying eyes above
One can get lost down here pretty easy
Seeking hidden dimensions in plain sight

TOMES OF OLD

Standing tall in formation
Rise forms appear and fade
Like saintly apparitions
Written in tomes of old

MOON AND STARS

Every day up is a miracle in the making
Ten billion years or maybe more who knows
Our ancestors having gotten us not very far
So I aim for the moon and shoot for the stars

PAST AND FUTURE

Living many lifetimes in one blink of an eye
Time stands still in the heat of any moment
When one exists only in this present tense
Past and future relinquish their control

WAY OF LIFE

Walking through realms
Of heavenly delight,
Looking for adventures
In dawn's early light.
You've put your time in
Anticipating the thrill,
Rewards hard to fathom
Rewards subtle yet real.
Some people may dare;
(It's too much like work)
But little do they comprehend
Intangibles beyond compare.
No – ours is a way of life
Not a way to make a living,
Though life wouldn't be as sweet
If we weren't able to share
His blessings and our giving.
There's not enough time
To waste on idle chatter,
So us fishers of trout and men
Give all that we've got
Because nothing else matters.

BROTHERS IN ARMS
Riding off into sunsets long ago
Leaving no trace or dust in the wind
Worlds away sitting on my porch safely
Brothers in arms below a red'n orange glow

THOSE WHO ASK
Small pictures are all that remains
Having left with some never returned
Floating within seas of life and change
I swim to the surface saving those who ask

MOUNTAIN MAJESTY
Past city's hectic pace
Beyond modern man's reach
Ten acres of mountain's majesty
With a shop out back for all my bros

KEEP THE PEACE

We parted last time in a blaze of glory
Distant countries practicing the art of war
Now that we've fulfilled our mission and more
Is there someone out there who can keep the peace

ULTIMATE REALITY

Countless eons of foggy minds still
Like a disturbed pond clarity is not
When one sits amidst ultimate reality
Knowing it is the hardest thing to see

MOSTLY GOOD

Troubled by everything I hear on the news
Sport of hidden forces spreading contention
Is there a billionaire somewhere in this world
Who'll create a network that extols mostly good

THIS YEAR

How many of you have bank accounts gushing
And idletime aplenty with more money to burn
Imagine if you called upon those closest to you
How many more enterprises could you foster this year

WAKE UP

Not so clean rivers run through many valleys
Skies that're filled with questionable air
I wonder if people learned to slow down
They'd wake up and change their course

HERE TO ETERNITY

Bees and birds visit their local pantry
With scents so bright and sweeter tastes too
If only we could decipher what they had to say
Our ears would probably burn from here to eternity

OUR POTENTIAL

Waiting for countless guests to arrive
Sitting on high they watch and listen
Offering subtle wisdom and insights
Hoping our potential is reached

THROUGH THE ROOF

As gray starts creeping around your hairline
And some mornings you may feel a little stiff
The mind begins to center becoming more aware
Levels of appreciation shoot through the roof

YOU OFFERED

Saute'd trout, mushrooms, bacon and onions
With a dash of garlic thrown in for measure
Reluctantly plucked from your world friend
But I'm try'in to save mine and you offered

TWO LEGS

Walking through nirvana all eyes are upon me
Foul, feathers, fur, critters of every sort
Watching with intent and wondering how
Those with two legs rarely tip over

EVERY DETAIL

Planting some seeds in our up and comers
Little diamonds in the rough for sure
With attention paid to every detail
So they can't say well you did it

PURE INTENTIONS

Cycles of life and death make their appearance
First hints of autumn are a welcome sensation
Hyperborean nights waiting in time's wheel
I'm buckling down with pure intentions

IF
With a sweet scent of hopes and dreams
Eternal visions in your still inner self
Slowing down enables you to appreciate much
Millions worth if someone could count that high

ETHEREAL WARRIORS
For many a moon since our return
Oceans away in cool rivers of belief
Me and my brothers standing in formation
Ethereal warriors fighting in realms unknown

WHAT REALLY MATTERS
Friends and families scattered across our land
Old ways of community blowing leaves in the wind
Ask yourself can we get back to what really matters
When the ground of being appears to be like a phantom

WHITE ROBES

One fast way to inner peace you know
Cooking with kindness equanimity grows
Carrying on with ways of the wise men do
Whether you happen to wear white robes or not

BEST LAID PLANS

Lives filled with anxiety frustrates
Even the best laid plans get fubar
When you become one with the way
The sleeper will be awakened

YELLOW BRICK ROADS

Leaning to your right two roads part
How it leads one rarely comprehends then
Heading onto paths where worn trod's gotten
Yellow brick roads in our galaxy knows no end

TO BE CALLED
Wild mountain peaks caressing the sky
A meeting place that has no compare
In boardrooms sits our Boss on high
And us faithful wait to be called

MY MIND
Sky beards dancing constant motions
Cotton candy floods furthest horizons
Feeling the magic that surrounds us all
While my mind comes to rest in complete awe

SEVEN DIRECTIONS
Traipsing through a maze in silver-green
Paths of life lived invisible and seen
The others have already headed out
From seven directions they come

TEST OF TIME

In rushing gorges where water cuts deeply
Mother earth complains but no one listens
Like me invisible forces assail my senses
Just like her I'll stand the test of time

LIVE AND FIGHT

Rivers rest flowing in early morning's light
Beings on daily searches to live and fight
Opening flaps from another restful sleep
Wondering am I awake or just dreaming

WARMER PASTURES

Old man winter sends his scouting party out
Fall chills rushing over areas of operation
With sounds of horns off to warmer pastures
Tugging on my parka I'm relishing this life

ANCIENT RACE

A cosmic guise sparkles and winks around campfire bright
For millennia myths have been carved on torch-lit walls
An ancient race attempting to comprehend mysteries
Many kalpas later still not much has changed

NEVER ENDING

Lavender clouds coat setting orb
Dim shadows begin to frolic and play
Perfect beginnings for those to witness
Neverending dance holding lifetime seats

CREEK FREEK

Ya you've got that jones for sure
Time to get while the get'ins good
Might be a half bubble off of plumb
A creek freek head'in for your woods

MOVE ALONG
Windswept valleys cut by glacial wizards
Our most recent ice age feels like last week
Big browns bickering over their favorite holes
Better keep moving along and watch these bullies

COSMIC PULSE
Silent steps fall in moonlit forests
So surreal I can feel the cosmic pulse
Another mile or two I'll make camp there
And try to figure out which reality I'm in

SEEMS LIKE
Back at the spot with grassy creel dripping
Waiting to see if my buddies brought back
Chopping some sticks setting them alight
Seems like I'm always the first to show

FAMILY MEMORIES

Underneath kaleidoscopes dazzling and razzling
Painted domes in Big Sky Country you'll see
Big browns'n cuttys rising rain or shine
And family memories are etched in time

BLUE SHIP

In nearby dimensions angels are sighing
Trying to hold back eagerness that shows
Mortals on a blue ship blazing in ignorance
Hoping sincerest of efforts were not in vain

PERFECT BEING

A luminous mother begins her sojourn
One of trillions orbiting its centers
Where life thrives, claws and scratches
Trying to develop into the perfect being

NEW TACK
Going to places where cascades fall call and echo
Clouds of mist roar like a pride of invisible lions
For eons and eons uprights having kept their status quo
Does anybody out there agree it's time to try a newer tack

WISE UP
Years and days rolling like tidal dancers
Gray-haired wrinkles follow their pull
Watching young ones grow like weeds
Better wise up without any delay

PERPETUAL MOTION
Stopping and starting like wind and rain
Uneven strokes have a tendency to dissuade
Perpetual motion on the harmony church train
How long will they tolerate limitless ignorance

WHAT DELIGHTS
Another day dawns beneath a red and orange hue
Fair market and organic we're making choices
While my skillet begins approaching degree
Wondering what delights I have in store

MAKE THEIR MARKS
If despair and hate ever overcomes
Lifetimes of oppression takes it toll
This is when the others make their marks
Putting your name in left or right columns

DAILY BASIS
Nearly knocking on His pearly gates
The stairway to heaven was quite near
Now I've settled into a brand new groove
Where I commune with nature on a daily basis

SOOTHES MY SOUL
Been there and back
By the skin of my strap
Clean mountain air
Really soothes my soul

EBB & FLOW
Between 9:00 and 2:00
Rhythms of life swinging
Like me in harmony humming
Playing with the ebb and flow

PRESENT DELIGHTS
I've been to the brink
Worry and doubt abounded
Having lost their hold on me
My mind floats on present delights

THOUGHTS OF COMPASSION
Last visit's done
No more scary outings
Now I concentrate and live
Casting thoughts of compassion

LONG STRANGE TRIP
Load'in up my overnight bag again
Each trip out is a further trip in
Leaving out shiny trinkets and things
Now I'm packing light for the long haul

WHERE I GO
Nature's pharmacy holds
Medicine beyond compare
It's where I usually go
To bring my balance back

NEW BEGINNING
Longer days and brighter nights
Drips and concoctions in white rooms
Been there done it, lived it, learned it
Although I can't really say that I loved it

WILL TRAVEL
Having been party to many scenes
Maneuvers under knife's glare
Got some new operations now
Have fly rod, will travel

PROSTHETIC DEVICES
I bit the old double whammy
A shocker from hills to dales
Sporting cute prosthetic devices
Things've really started to perk up

OUR UNIT
Finally back with family and friends
Surely they must've read it by now
Luckily there were no reporters
Imbedded within our unit

UNDER YOUR NOSE
Seeking and searching hidden realms
Diligently contemplating conundrums
Roads to heaven are under your nose
Actually you're already on them

LIKE I DO
My favorite jewel set amongst stones
Sparkles and shimmers dazzling my mind
Show me a mortal who creates such beauty
If only my wife would see things like I do

ROAR AND CHIRP
Brita filters could help
For all who drink and live
Your shiny little birds
Who roar instead of chirp

MORE SIMPLE
Back in days of old
When tales were taller
Life was much more simple
Why didn't we pass the tests

LAST POEM
Many years after pain hasn't stopped
Trips'n missions linger down deep
Finally found these magical keys
And the last poem in my book

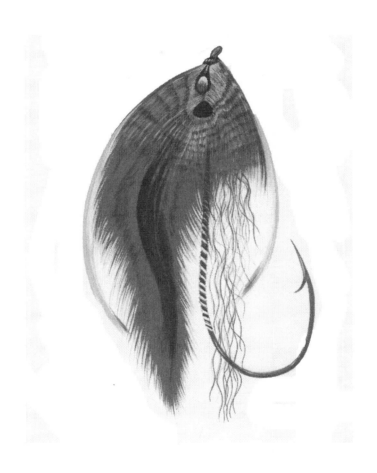

AUTHOR'S LIBRARY STARTER KIT LIST

1. A Search For God Bk. I & II Paraphrased — L. Nelson Farley
2. A Path With Heart — Jack Kornfield
3. Autobiography Of A Yogi — Paramahansa Yogananda
4. The Inner Life — Hazrat Inayat Khan
5. Seat Of The Soul — Gary Zukav
6. The Road Less Travelled — M. Scott Peck
7. The Way Of The Peaceful Warrior — Dan Millman
8. In Defense Of Poetry — P.B. Shelley
9. Letters To A Young Poet — R.M. Rilke
10. Poetic Medicine — John Fox
11. The Right To Write — Julia Cameron
12. Deep Trout — William Washabaugh
13. If I Could Scream — Paul Schullery
14. Studies In The Sermon On The Mount — D. Martyn Lloyd-Jones
15. Mystery Of The Ages — Herbert W. Armstrong

PRODIGAL SONS

Caught in this web of thieves and fools
With other unfortunates who've lost their way,
Every day lived is another day blessed
Myriad opportunites for those who can see.
State-sanctioned killings now and then
Acts unspeakable committed with delusion,
A heavy price paid from one wrong to another
How many more years will it take to learn?
Spirits in a material world trying to cope
Democratic principles is our claim to fame,
Once one sits down to ponder ancient paths
Invisible wisdom begins to dawn.
A life given from an uncreated beginning
With destiny laid out of unknown origin,
Who knows if an eye for an eye
Is conducive for humans on the noble path?
Time to reflect and atone for one's wrongs
Idle minds are fury's favorite friends,
All actions must bear fruit
So watch your thoughts
And hold your tongues—
For it is deeds that speak
Sealing the fates of
Many a prodigal son.

SURELY WE MUST

Standing on a precipice
Sacred horizons with vast potential,
Do we call out sentient beings
Gently gathering all supporters
In a concerted effort
To save some souls.
In this cosmic scheme
We defy all perceptions,
State-sanctioned killings
One wrong begets another,
Who on earth can calculate
Odds without logic?
Troubled youth set in motion
Confused minds and heavy hearts,
Can anyone forgive ourselves
Letting this sad state of affairs
Propagate such unwanted fruit?
Duties and conundrums with
Pedigrees'n Ph.Ds
Trying to figure out
What went wrong?
Left turns on long paths gone
Socio-economic oppression
Condoned by those at the helm,
Surely we must do better
If we're ever to live up to
And exceed otherworldly expectations.

WHO EVER THOUGHT?

Looking out into
A maze of confusion,
Hate and revenge
Gone awry,
Who ever thought
One wrong would
Put another wrong right?
An evolving species said to be
For thousands of years or more,
How dare anyone say
We are almost ready!
In distant lands and
Unseen dimensions,
Do I laugh or cry
After the pronouncement's made?
Political chaos reigns then
Muddled minds weigh
The fate of nations
And slightly lost souls,
Who ever thought we'd
Stoop so low?

WARNING!!!

Now that you all have enjoyed this treat, please use your supernatural gifts to create a better world while we still have a fighting chance.

To all my soldiers, sinners and saints, there are no excuses now, so go make it happen!

For booking and information,
visit www.poetryinmotions.org
or email us at
poetryinmotions@outlook.com

Made in the USA
Columbia, SC
20 May 2021